It's another Quality Book from CGP

This book has been carefully written for 8-9 year olds.

There's lots of stuff to learn in the Year 4 Maths Programme of Study. Happily, this CGP book explains it all as clearly and simply as possible.

What's more, it's perfectly matched to the National Curriculum for 2014 and beyond.

What CGP is all about

Our sole aim here at CGP is to produce the highest quality books — carefully written, immaculately presented and dangerously close to being funny.

Then we work our socks off to get them out to you — at the cheapest possible prices.

Contents

Section Four — Measurement

Section Five — Geometry

Section Six — Statistics

Published by CGP

Editors:
Katie Braid, Katherine Craig, Ben Fletcher, Sarah Pattison, Camilla Simson, Sean Stayte.

ISBN: 978 1 84762 191 7

With thanks to Karen Wells and Nicola Paddock for the proofreading.
With thanks to Jan Greenway for the copyright research.

Thumb illustration used throughout the book © iStockphoto.com.

Contains public sector information licensed under the Open Government Licence v2.0.
http://www.nationalarchives.gov.uk/doc/open-government-licence/

Printed by Elanders Ltd, Newcastle upon Tyne.
Clipart from Corel®

Based on the classic CGP style created by Richard Parsons.

About This Book

This Book has All the Topics for Year 4

By the end of Year 4, you should be able to do all the maths in this book.

Each page covers a different topic, with examples to help explain the maths.

This book covers the Attainment Targets for Year 4 of the 2014 National Curriculum. The topics covered are roughly equivalent to the old Levels 3-4.

Examples are colour-coded to show the difficulty of problems in a topic.

EXAMPLE: Easy   **EXAMPLE:** Harder   **EXAMPLE:** Challenge

At the end of each section are practice questions.
You can see what you know and what you need to work on.

These questions are colour-coded too, to help you pick which ones to tackle.

Key:
Easy Start
Getting Harder
Challenge

This Study Book has a matching Question Book.
It's got questions on all the topics and some practice tests too.

There are Learning Objectives on All Pages

Learning objectives say what you should be able to do.
Use the tick circles to show how confident you feel.

I can win gold at the Olympics.

You can use the tick boxes for ongoing assessment to record which attainment targets have been met. Printable checklists of all the objectives can be found at www.cgpbooks.co.uk/primarymaths.

Tick here if you think you need a bit more practice.

If you're really struggling, tick here.

Tick this circle if you can do all the maths on the page.

"I can multiply and divide using my times tables."

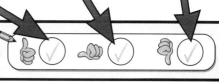

Counting in Multiples

Use Number Lines to Count On in Steps

You can use number lines to <u>count on</u>. You can count in ones: 0, 1, 2, 3...
Or you could count in steps of <u>other numbers</u>. Go <u>six steps</u> at a time:

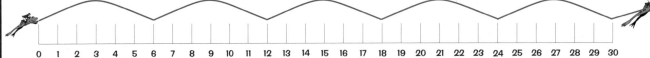

0 1 2 3 4 5 6 7 8 9 10 11 12 13 14 15 16 17 18 19 20 21 22 23 24 25 26 27 28 29 30

Starting from zero you get: 0, 6, 12, 18, 24, 30... This is <u>counting in sixes</u>.
The numbers you get (after zero) are called <u>multiples</u> of six.

Times Tables for 6, 7 and 9

The best way to count up in multiples of <u>6, 7 and 9</u> is to learn their <u>times tables</u>:

$1 \times 6 = 6$	$1 \times 7 = 7$	$1 \times 9 = 9$
$2 \times 6 = 12$	$2 \times 7 = 14$	$2 \times 9 = 18$
$3 \times 6 = 18$	$3 \times 7 = 21$	$3 \times 9 = 27$
$4 \times 6 = 24$	$4 \times 7 = 28$	$4 \times 9 = 36$
$5 \times 6 = 30$	$5 \times 7 = 35$	$5 \times 9 = 45$
$6 \times 6 = 36$	$6 \times 7 = 42$	$6 \times 9 = 54$
$7 \times 6 = 42$	$7 \times 7 = 49$	$7 \times 9 = 63$
$8 \times 6 = 48$	$8 \times 7 = 56$	$8 \times 9 = 72$
$9 \times 6 = 54$	$9 \times 7 = 63$	$9 \times 9 = 81$
$10 \times 6 = 60$	$10 \times 7 = 70$	$10 \times 9 = 90$
MULTIPLES OF 6	MULTIPLES OF 7	MULTIPLES OF 9

Counting in 25s and 1000s

<u>Multiples of 1000</u> are easy
— count in <u>1s</u> but say '<u>thousand</u>'
(and write '<u>000</u>').

1000 2000 3000 4000...

1st digit goes up by 1.

Now, <u>multiples of 25</u>. There are <u>4 lots of 25 in every 100</u> —
there's a <u>25</u>, <u>50</u> and <u>75</u> between each hundred.

25 50 75 100 125 150 175 200 225 250 275 300

There's a 25, 50 and
75 in the first hundred...

...and the second hundred...

...and all the other hundreds.

"I can count in multiples of 6, 7, 9, 25 and 1000."

Counting Backwards Through Zero

Negatives on the Number Line

The number line is really useful for understanding negative numbers.

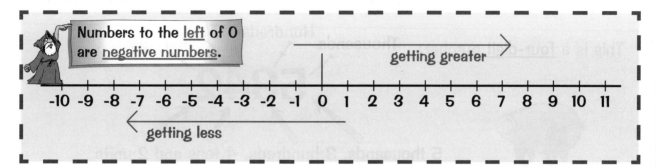

Numbers to the left of 0 are negative numbers.

getting greater

-10 -9 -8 -7 -6 -5 -4 -3 -2 -1 0 1 2 3 4 5 6 7 8 9 10 11

getting less

On the number line, the further right you go, the greater the numbers get.

It's easy to think that -7 is greater than -4 because 7 is greater than 4. But...

-7 is less than -4 because it's further to the left on the number line.

You Can Count Back with a Number Line

EXAMPLE: Count back in threes from 5.
If you can't do this in your head, a number line is helpful.

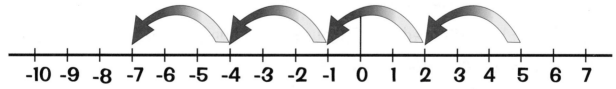

-10 -9 -8 -7 -6 -5 -4 -3 -2 -1 0 1 2 3 4 5 6 7

Start at 5 and jump backwards in steps of 3.
So it goes 5, 2, –1, –4, –7...

"I can count back through zero using negative numbers."

Place Value and Partitioning

All Numbers are Made of Digits

A <u>digit</u> is any one of these:　0 1 2 3 4 5 6 7 8 9

This is a <u>four-digit</u> number:

Thousands Hundreds Tens Units

5342

5 thousands, 3 hundreds, 4 tens and 2 units

"five thousand three hundred and forty-two"

Place Value

The <u>value</u> of a digit depends on its <u>place</u> in the number.

The digit on the <u>right</u> is always the <u>units</u>.

Then it's the <u>tens</u>.

Then it's the <u>hundreds</u>.

Then it's the <u>thousands</u>.

Three-digit numbers don't have any thousands.

Th H T U
3 4 2
7 6 5 8

Numbers Can Be Partitioned

Partitioning is breaking up numbers.

<u>2842</u> can be partitioned into <u>2 thousands</u>, <u>8 hundreds</u>, <u>4 tens</u> and <u>2 units</u>.

So 2842 = 2000 + 800 + 40 + 2.

Or you could do it like this...　2000 + 800 + 30 + 12

Or this...　2000 + 830 + 10 + 2

"I know the place value of each digit in a four-digit number (thousands, hundreds, tens and units)."

1000 More or Less

Finding 1000 More

To find the number that is <u>1000 more</u> than another number,
<u>add 1 to the thousands</u>.

EXAMPLES:

What number is 1000 more than 5992?

Add 1 to the
thousands.
↘ **5992**

Answer: **6992**

What is 4562 + 1000?

Add 1 to the
thousands.
↘ **4562**

Answer: **5562**

What number is
<u>1000 more</u> than <u>169</u>?

It's a three-digit number
so there are 0 thousands. → **0169**   Answer: **1169**

Finding 1000 Less

To get <u>1000 less</u>, <u>take 1 away</u> from the <u>thousands</u>.

EXAMPLE:

What number is 1000 less than 2350?

Take 1 away from
the thousands. ↘ **2350**

Answer: **1350**

EXAMPLE:

What is 20 462 – 1000?

This is 20 thousands,
4 hundreds, 6 tens
and 2 units.

You can't take 1 from 0. ↗ **20 462**
But you can take 1 (thousand) from 20 (thousand)...

...take 1 from 20, leaving 19. ↘ **20 462**

Answer: **19 462**

"I can find 1000 more than a number,
and 1000 less than a number."

Ordering and Comparing Numbers

Ordering Numbers

Four-digit numbers are bigger than three-digit numbers.
Three-digit numbers are bigger than two-digit numbers.
One-digit numbers are the smallest.

EXAMPLE:

6666 is bigger than **777**, which is bigger than **88**, which is bigger than **9**.

To put numbers with the same number of digits in size order,
compare them digit by digit.

EXAMPLE: Order these numbers from smallest to largest: 3491, 3291, 3284.

Look at the first digit of each number.	3491, 3291, 3284
They're all the same so look at the next digit along.	3491, 3291, 3284
3491 has the biggest 2nd digit, so put it at the end.	3291, 3284, 3491

This is because 3400 is bigger than 3200.

The first two numbers have the same second digit.
So you have to look at their third digits.   3291, 3284, 3491

90 is bigger than 80, so swap the two numbers around.   3284, 3291, 3491

And that's it. So the correct order is 3284, 3291, 3491.

Use < and > to Compare Numbers

Inequalities use the
symbols < and >.

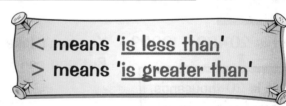

< means 'is less than'
> means 'is greater than'

For example, 5892 > 5738
means '5892 is greater than 5738'.

"I can put four-digit numbers in order,
and use the < and > symbols."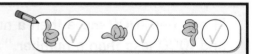

Rounding

Rounding Numbers

You can <u>round</u> numbers to the <u>nearest</u> 10, 100 or 1000.
For example, here's how to round 342 to the nearest 100:

342 is <u>between two possible answers</u>: 300 and 400.
You need to choose the <u>nearest one</u>.

If the number is exactly in the middle of the two possible answers then round it <u>up</u>.

350 is <u>halfway between</u> 300 and 400.
342 is <u>less</u> than halfway, so it's closer to 300 than 400. This means you <u>round down</u>.

So 342 rounded to the nearest 100 is <u>300</u>.

EXAMPLES:

a) Round 237 to the nearest 10.

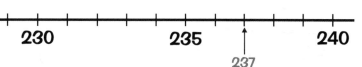

2<u>3</u>7 is between 2<u>30</u> and 2<u>40</u>. It's closer to 240, so the answer is <u>240</u>.

b) Round 4499 to the nearest 1000.

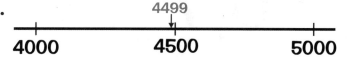

<u>4499</u> is between <u>4000</u> and <u>5000</u>.
It's slightly closer to 4000 — it's 499 above 4000, but 501 below 5000.
So the answer is <u>4000</u>.

EXAMPLE:

Paul rounded a number to the <u>nearest 100</u>. The answer is <u>400</u>.
What numbers could he have started with?

Any number from 350 upwards will round up to 400. Any number below 450 will round down to 400. So the number is <u>between 350 and 449</u>.

"I can round numbers to the nearest 10, 100 or 1000."

Decimal Numbers and Fractions

Fractions Show Numbers That Aren't Whole...

Numbers that are <u>not whole numbers</u> can be written as <u>fractions</u>.
For example, <u>three quarters</u>:

The <u>bottom number</u> is the <u>denominator</u>. It tells you <u>how many equal parts</u> something is split into.

3
―
4

The <u>top number</u> is the <u>numerator</u>. It tells you <u>how many</u> of those equal parts you've got. (So this is 3 out of 4.)

Here's a <u>fraction bar</u> for ¾ — it has <u>3 parts</u> shaded <u>out of 4</u>.

...and so do Decimals

Numbers that <u>aren't whole numbers</u> can be written as <u>decimals</u>. Decimals all have a <u>decimal point</u> in them — this just looks like a full stop. As well as having units, tens, hundreds, etc., decimals can also have <u>tenths</u>, <u>hundredths</u> and <u>thousandths</u>. These are all worth <u>less than 1</u>.

EXAMPLES:

<u>0.7</u> is between 0 and 1.
It's said as '<u>nought</u> point <u>seven</u>'.

Units Tenths

0.7

Digits to the right of the decimal point are worth less than 1.

Decimal point   <u>7 tenths</u>

<u>1.35</u> is between 1 and 2.
It's said as '<u>one</u> point <u>three five</u>'.

Units Tenths Hundredths

1.35

<u>1 unit</u>   <u>3 tenths</u>   <u>5 hundredths</u>

They Can Both go on the Number Line

You can use <u>number lines</u> to show the <u>sizes</u> of <u>decimal numbers</u> and <u>fractions</u>.

Each <u>big division</u> here is a <u>tenth</u>.

0   0.1 0.2 0.3 0.4 0.5 0.6 0.7 0.8 0.9   1   1.1 1.2 1.3 ↓1.4

1.35

One <u>tiny division</u> is a <u>hundredth</u>.

Each of the big divisions is 1 tenth. 0 $\frac{1}{10}$ $\frac{2}{10}$ $\frac{3}{10}$ $\frac{4}{10}$ $\frac{5}{10}$ $\frac{6}{10}$ $\frac{7}{10}$ $\frac{8}{10}$ $\frac{9}{10}$ 1

Some other common fractions. $\frac{1}{4}$ $\frac{1}{3}$ $\frac{1}{2}$ $\frac{2}{3}$ $\frac{3}{4}$

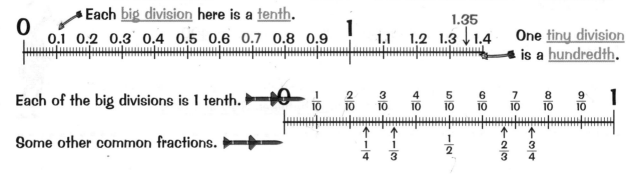

"I know that numbers which aren't whole numbers can be written as decimals or fractions."

Roman Numerals

The Romans Used Letters to Show Numbers

Instead of the digits 0, 1, 2, 3, 4, 5, 6, 7, 8 and 9 the Romans
used letters called Roman numerals. Here are the first few:

$$I = 1 \quad V = 5 \quad X = 10 \quad L = 50 \quad C = 100$$

They didn't use place value — each numeral always means the same amount.
They also didn't have a letter for zero. These things came later.

Numerals Put Together Make Other Numbers

For numbers they didn't have a numeral for (like 2), they put numerals together...

More than one of the same numeral in a row means add them together.

I sword	II swords	X swords	XXX swords
1 sword	1 + 1 = 2	10 swords	10 + 10 + 10 = 30

A small numeral after a bigger one also means add them together.

A small numeral before a bigger one means you subtract the small one from the bigger one.

Do any subtracting first, before you do any adding.

 VIII swords
5 + 1 + 1 + 1 = 8

 LX
50 + 10 = 60

IV swords
5 – 1 = 4

 XL
50 – 10 = 40

 XIV
5 – 1 = 4
10 + 4 = 14

Here are some more numbers and their Roman numerals:

3 III	9 IX	24 XXIV	51 LI	90 XC
6 VI	20 XX	42 XLII	61 LXI	95 XCV

"I can read Roman numerals up to 100. I know that
Roman numerals don't have zeros or place value."

Solving Number Problems

Work Out What Calculation You Need to Do

EXAMPLE: Rachel swims 6 lengths of a pool that is 25 metres long.
How many metres does she swim?

You need to work out what <u>six lots of 25</u> are.
You could do this by <u>counting on</u> in 25s six times:

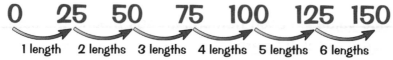

0   25   50   75   100   125   150
1 length 2 lengths 3 lengths 4 lengths 5 lengths 6 lengths

So she swims <u>150 metres</u>.

EXAMPLE: The temperature in John's freezer was 1 °C.
It's now 7 °C colder. What temperature is it now?

You need to <u>start at 1</u> and <u>count back 7</u>. You could use a number line:

-10 -9 -8 -7 -6 -5 -4 -3 -2 -1 0 1 2

So the answer is –6 °C.

Some Problems Have More Than One Step

EXAMPLE:

Naz tiles the wall alongside his bath, plus 1000 mm more of the wall.
His bath is 1725 mm long. To the nearest 100 mm, what length of wall
does he tile?

First you need to <u>add 1000</u>
to 1725, so find the
<u>thousands digit</u> and <u>add one</u>.

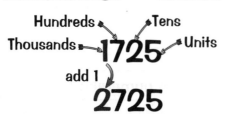

Hundreds   Tens
Thousands   **1725**   Units
add 1
2725

Then you need to <u>round</u> 2725 to
the <u>nearest 100</u>.
2725 is between 2700 and 2800:

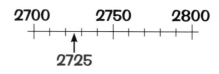

2700   2750   2800

2725

2725 is closer to 2700,
so it rounds to <u>2700 mm</u>.

"I can solve problems with negative numbers
and with large numbers."

Solving Number Problems

Some Problems Use Fractions...

EXAMPLE:

Hannah has a chocolate bar with 5 segments. She gives 2 segments to Lizzi.

a) What fraction of the chocolate bar did she give to Lizzi?

> If something is divided into <u>5 equal parts</u>, then the <u>denominator</u> is 5:
>
> $$\frac{2}{5}$$
>
> Lizzi gets <u>2 of the 5</u> pieces, so the <u>numerator</u> is 2, and the <u>answer</u> is $\frac{2}{5}$.

b) What fraction of the chocolate bar does she have left?

> It can help to <u>draw a fraction bar</u>. There are <u>5 pieces</u> in total, so <u>split it into 5</u>:
>
> $\frac{5}{5} = 1$
>
> Lizzi has <u>2 pieces</u>.
>
> 5 – 2 = 3, so there are <u>3 pieces left</u>, and the <u>answer</u> is $\frac{3}{5}$.

...and Some Problems Use Scales

Treat a <u>scale</u> like a <u>number line</u>...

EXAMPLE: How <u>long</u> is the giant centipede, to the <u>nearest 10 cm</u>?

Each small division on this ruler is 1 cm.

The nearest big divisions are <u>20 cm</u> and <u>30 cm</u>. So the length is <u>between 20 and 30 cm</u>.

Each big division is 10 cm.

Halfway between is 25 cm. The length is <u>nearer</u> to <u>20 cm</u> than 30 cm.

> Answer: The centipede is <u>20 cm long</u> to the <u>nearest 10 cm</u>.

"I can solve problems using fractions and rounding."

SECTION ONE — NUMBER AND PLACE VALUE

Practice Questions

Start off with the green questions — they're the easiest ones.
The blue ones are a bit harder, and the pink ones are the hardest.

1   What are the next three multiples of seven?

         7   14   21   28...

2   Starting at 2000, count on to 6000 in steps of 1000.

3   What number is 1000 more than...

         a)   881   b)   3465   c)   8262

4   Work out what 4 minus 11 is. Use a number line to help you.

5   How many thousands are in the each of these numbers?

         a)   4529   b)   683   c)   1989

6   Partition each number into thousands, hundreds, tens and units.

         a)   3346   b)   2587   c)   4002

7   What number is 1000 less than...

         a)   9881?   b)   3259?   c)   1589?

8   Round these numbers:

         a)   176 to the nearest 10   b)   6359 to the nearest 1000

9   Starting at 150, count in multiples of 25. Stop at 250.

10   What numbers do these Roman numerals show?

         a)   LV   b)   IX   c)   XXIV

Practice Questions

11 The numbers in this sequence increase by 3 each time.
Fill in the missing numbers. Use a number line to help you.

−14 ☐ ☐ ☐ −2 1 −14

12 Copy these sentences. Put a < or > in each box to make them correct.

a) 500 ☐ 459   b) 619 ☐ 691   c) 1099 ☐ 1100

d) −5 ☐ −8   e) −7 ☐ 6   f) 908 ☐ 1160

13 Brian has 8549 eagles in his zoo. 1000 eagles leave to go to Mr Sea's circus.

How many eagles does Brian have left, rounded to the nearest:

a) 1000?   b) 100?   c) 10?

14 Declan threw a javelin. He measured from where he threw it to where it landed.

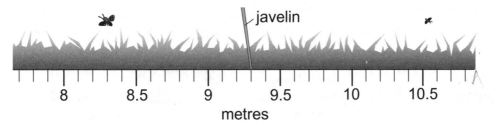

javelin

8   8.5   9   9.5   10   10.5
metres

a) How far did Declan throw the javelin?

b) Antony the Roman threw a javelin XI metres.
Who threw the javelin further, Declan or Antony?

15 The thermometer shows the temperature in Jack's cold room.

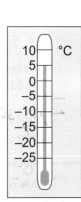

a) What is the current temperature?

b) What is the current temperature, rounded to the nearest 10 °C?

c) Jack turns the temperature down by 15 °C.
What will the new temperature be?

Written Addition

You Can Add In Columns

| EXAMPLE: | Work out <u>2381 + 1556</u> without using a calculator. |

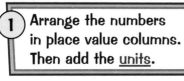
1 Arrange the numbers in place value columns. Then add the <u>units</u>.

```
Th H T U
 2  3 8 1
+1  5 5 6
         7
```
1 + 6 = 7

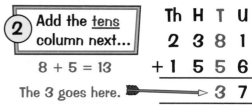
2 Add the <u>tens</u> column next...

```
Th H T U
 2  3 8 1
+1  5 5 6
       3 7
```
8 + 5 = 13

The 3 goes here.

10 tens = 100. So put 100 below the hundreds column. 1

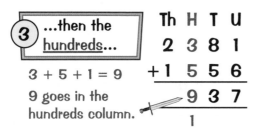
3 ...then the <u>hundreds</u>...

3 + 5 + 1 = 9

9 goes in the hundreds column.
```
Th H T U
 2  3 8 1
+1  5 5 6
    9 3 7
   1
```

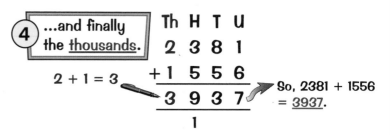
4 ...and finally the <u>thousands</u>.

2 + 1 = 3
```
Th H T U
 2  3 8 1
+1  5 5 6
 3  9 3 7
   1
```
So, 2381 + 1556 = <u>3937</u>.

You Can Add Decimals in the Same Way

| EXAMPLE: | Work out <u>23.83 + 35.4</u> |

See page 28 for more on decimals.

When you write the numbers down, always <u>line up the decimal points</u>. Then start adding, beginning with the place value column of <u>least value</u> (it's always on the right).

1 Add the <u>hundredths</u>.
```
T U t h
2 3.8 3
+3 5.4 0
    . 3
```
You can put in a zero here, to show there are no hundredths.

Always put the decimal point in first.   3 + 0 = 3

2 Add the <u>tenths</u>.
```
T U t h
2 3.8 3
+3 5.4 0
   .2 3
  1
```
8 + 4 = 12

10 tenths = 1. Put 1 below the units column.

3 Add the <u>units</u>.
```
T U t h
2 3.8 3
+3 5.4 0
  9.2 3
 1
```
3 + 5 + 1 = 9

Remember to add this 1 too.

4 Add the <u>tens</u>.
```
T U t h
2 3.8 3
+3 5.4 0
5 9.2 3
```
To finish, add up the last column.

2 + 3 = 5

So 23.83 + 35.4 = <u>59.23</u>
(Don't forget the decimal point.)

"I can add numbers with up to four digits using a written method."

Written Subtraction

In Subtractions, You May Need to Exchange

You set out <u>subtractions</u> the same way as additions. Line up the <u>units</u> or <u>decimal points</u>. Then you start subtracting with the column of <u>least place value</u>.

EXAMPLE: What is <u>9835 – 1216</u>?

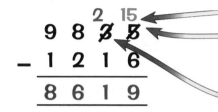

You can't do 5 – 6 because 6 is bigger than 5.

But you can <u>exchange</u> a <u>ten</u> from the 30 for <u>10 units</u>. Add those 10 units onto the 5 to make 15. Then 15 – 6 = <u>9</u>.

There's <u>10 less</u> here because you changed a ten into units.

EXAMPLE: Work out <u>83 – 9.6</u> without using a calculator.

(1) Line up the decimal points.

$$\begin{array}{ccc} T & U & t \\ 8 & 3 . & 0 \\ - & 9 . & 6 \\ \hline & . & \end{array}$$

<u>83</u> means <u>83.0</u>

(2) <u>Subtract the TENTHS</u>. You can't do 0 – 6, so exchange one of the <u>units</u> for 10 tenths. Then 10 – 6 = 4.

$$\begin{array}{ccc} T & U & t \\ 8 & 3.^2 & {}^1\bar{0} \\ - & 9 . & 6 \\ \hline & . & 4 \end{array}$$

(3) <u>Subtract the UNITS</u>. You can't do 2 – 9, so exchange a <u>ten</u> for 10 units. Then 12 – 9 = 3.

$$\begin{array}{ccc} T & U & t \\ 8^7 & {}_3{}^{12} . & {}^1 0 \\ - & 9 . & 6 \\ \hline & 3 . & 4 \end{array}$$

(4) <u>Subtract the TENS</u>. 7 – 0 = 7

$$\begin{array}{ccc} T & U & t \\ 8^7 & {}_3{}^{12} . & {}^1 0 \\ - & 9 . & 6 \\ \hline 7 & 3 . & 4 \end{array}$$

You Can Exchange Across Several Columns

Subtracting from a number with <u>zeros</u> in is a bit harder.

$$\begin{array}{c} 2\ 0\ 3 \\ -\ 1\ 1\ 6 \\ \hline \end{array}$$

You can't do 3 – 6. But there are <u>no tens</u> to exchange for 10 units...

...so you'll have to exchange a <u>hundred</u> for <u>10 tens</u>.

$$\begin{array}{c} 1 \quad {}^9{\cancel{10}}^1 \\ {\cancel{2}}{\cancel{0}}\ 3 \\ -\ 1\ 1\ 6 \\ \hline 8\ 7 \end{array}$$

Then exchange a <u>ten</u> for <u>10 units</u>. So you have <u>9 tens</u> left.

Now you have 13 units. 13 – 6 = 7

1 – 1 = 0   9 – 1 = 8

"I can subtract numbers with up to four digits using a written method."

Estimating and Checking

It's easy to make mistakes. So you should always <u>check your answers</u>.

Do the Inverse Operation...

EXAMPLE: Fred works out <u>72 – 32</u>. His answer is 50.
He can <u>check</u> it by doing the <u>inverse operation</u>.

<u>Inverse</u> just means <u>opposite</u>.

The inverse of "<u>– 32</u>" is "<u>+ 32</u>".
Fred should do <u>50 + 32</u> and see if he gets <u>72</u>.

<u>ADDITION</u> and <u>SUBTRACTION</u> are <u>inverse operations</u>.

50 + 32 = <u>82</u>

Fred was expecting to get <u>72</u>, so his answer of 50 <u>must be wrong</u>.

<u>MULTIPLICATION</u> and <u>DIVISION</u> are <u>inverse operations</u>.

...Or Estimate by Rounding Up or Down

You can check an answer by comparing it to an <u>estimate</u>.

EXAMPLE: Mary works out that <u>38 + 49 = 87</u>.
To check this, she can do an estimate to get a <u>rough answer</u>.

I'm only 87...

Round each number in the sum to the nearest 10.

38 is about **40**
49 is about **50**

Add the rounded numbers together. → 40 + 50 = 90

So ⟹ 38 + 49 is <u>about 90</u>

So Mary's answer of <u>87</u> seems <u>fine</u>. It's <u>probably right</u>.

Check that Your Answer is Sensible

Always <u>read your answer</u> and see if it <u>makes sense</u>.

"The <u>bus</u> is <u>2.5 m</u> high." ← This is <u>OK</u>.

The <u>pencil</u> is <u>2 m</u> long.
This <u>can't be right</u>.
You don't get 2 metre long pencils.

"I can make estimates and use inverse calculations to check my answers."

Using Times Tables

Learn Your Times Tables

You need to <u>know your times tables</u> up to <u>12 × 12</u>.
Here are a few ways you can remember some of them.

Multiples of 10 end in a '0'.
10   20   30   40   50 ...

Multiples of 5 end
in a '5' or a '0'.
5   10   15   20   25 ...

Multiples of <u>even</u> numbers
<u>end</u> in <u>even numbers</u>.
4   8   12   16   20 ...

Multiples of 9

9
18
27
36
45 ...

The tens go
up from 0 to 9.

It's always 1 less than the
number you're multiplying by.

The units go down
from 9 to 0.

The <u>digits add up to 9</u>.
This works for
<u>all multiples of 9</u>
up to 10 × 9 = 90.

1 + 8 = 9
2 + 7 = 9
3 + 6 = 9
4 + 5 = 9...

Dividing is the Inverse of Multiplying

Multiply 3 by 6 and you get 18.

Divide 18 by 6 and you get 3 again.

$3 \times 6 = 18$

$18 \div 6 = 3$

You can use your <u>times tables</u> to help you <u>divide</u>.

EXAMPLE: Divide fifty six by seven.

$56 \div 7 = ?$

You want to divide by 7.
So look at the 7 times table.

$8 \times 7 = 56$

So $56 \div 7 = \underline{8}$

"I know my times tables up to 12 × 12 and
can use them to multiply and divide."

Mental Multiplying and Dividing

Multiplying and Dividing by 1 and 0

A number doesn't change if you <u>multiply it by 1</u>.

EXAMPLE: What is 5 × 1?

$$5 × 1 = \underline{5}$$

You've only got <u>1 lot</u> of 5, so the answer is just 5.

A number also stays the same when <u>divided by 1</u>.

EXAMPLE: What is 5 ÷ 1?

$$5 ÷ 1 = \underline{5}$$

You're <u>splitting 5</u> into just one group, so the answer is 5.

Any number <u>multiplied by zero</u> becomes zero.

EXAMPLE: What is 5 × 0?

$$5 × 0 = \underline{0}$$

This time you have <u>no lots</u> of five, so the answer is zero.

You can Multiply Three Numbers Together

Break the multiplication down into easy steps. For example, for 2 × 7 × 3...

First multiply two of the numbers together...

$$2 × 3 = 6$$

$$6 × 7 = \underline{42}$$

...then multiply the answer by the third number.

(You could have done 2 × 7 = 14, but then you'd have to do 14 × 3, which is harder than 6 × 7.)

Use Easy Calculations to Solve Harder Ones

EXAMPLE: What is 600 ÷ 3?

You may not know what 600 ÷ 3 is...

...but you do know what 6 ÷ 3 is.

600 is 100 times bigger than 6, so the answer to 600 ÷ 3 will be 100 times bigger than the answer to 6 ÷ 3.

$$600 ÷ 3 = ?$$

$$6 ÷ 3 = 2$$

$$600 ÷ 3 = \underline{200}$$

"I can mentally multiply and divide numbers."

Factor Pairs

Factors of a Number Divide Into the Number

The <u>factors</u> of a number are <u>whole numbers</u> that <u>divide exactly into</u> that number.
<u>Two factors</u> that <u>multiply together</u> to give the number are called a <u>factor pair</u>.

HOW TO FIND FACTORS

1) Starting with 1, work out what you have to <u>times</u> that number by to make the number you're after.
   E.g. for 24, 1 × 24 = 24.
2) Then carry on with 2, 3, 4, etc.
3) If you <u>can't</u> find a number to make a factor pair then it's <u>not a factor</u>.
   E.g. 4 × 5 = 20, 5 × 5 = 25.
   So 5 isn't a factor of 24.
4) Keep going until you <u>repeat</u> a pair you've already got.

EXAMPLE: Find the factors of 24.

<u>ANSWER</u>: Start with 1 and work up:

$1 \times 24 = 24$
$2 \times 12 = 24$
$3 \times 8 = 24$
$4 \times 6 = 24$
$5 \times ? = ✗$
$6 \times 4 = 24$

This is the same as 4 × 6 so you can stop here.

So the factors of 24 are
<u>1</u>, <u>2</u>, <u>3</u>, <u>4</u>, <u>6</u>, <u>8</u>, <u>12</u> and <u>24</u>.

<u>Factors</u> can be written as factor pairs. For example:

The factor pairs of 24 are <u>1 and 24</u>, <u>2 and 12</u>, <u>3 and 8</u>, and <u>4 and 6</u>.

The <u>smallest</u> factor makes a pair with the <u>biggest</u> one...   ...the <u>second smallest</u> with the <u>second biggest</u>...   ...and so on.

Check they're factor pairs by multiplying them. $1 \times 24 = 24$, $3 \times 8 = 24$.

You can Multiply in Any Order

You can say: 2 rows of 3 apples...

2 × 3

...or 3 columns of 2 apples...

3 × 2

...but the answer is still <u>6</u>.

EXAMPLE: Jack plants 3 magic beans in every pot.
He has 4 pots. How many seeds does he plant?

You need to work out $4 \times 3 = ?$

You can get the answer using the 4 times table if you can't remember the 3 times table.

$4 \times 3 = 3 \times 4 = \underline{12}$

"I can recognise and use factor pairs in calculations."

Written Multiplication

Multiplying by a One-Digit Integer

> Integer just means a whole number.

1) Write out the calculation with the <u>big number on top</u>. Line up the place value columns.

2) Multiply the <u>one-digit</u> number by <u>each part</u> of the big number in turn. Start with the place value column of <u>least</u> value (it's always the one on the right).

3) Each time you get an answer of 10 or more, <u>record</u> the first digit of the answer below the next column (like you do when you're adding).

EXAMPLE: Work out 167 × 4 without using a calculator.

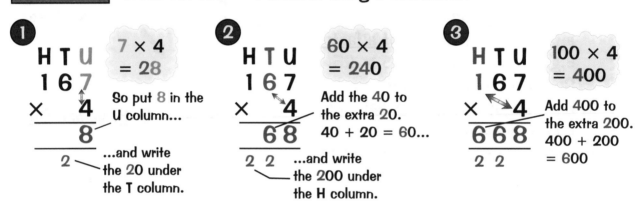

①
```
  H T U
  1 6 7
×     4
─────────
      8
    2
```
7 × 4 = 28
So put 8 in the U column...
...and write the 20 under the T column.

②
```
  H T U
  1 6 7
×     4
─────────
    6 8
  2 2
```
60 × 4 = 240
Add the 40 to the extra 20. 40 + 20 = 60...
...and write the 200 under the H column.

③
```
  H T U
  1 6 7
×     4
─────────
  6 6 8
  2 2
```
100 × 4 = 400
Add 400 to the extra 200. 400 + 200 = 600

EXAMPLE: Alice buys 5 vats of pickles. Each vat contains exactly 274 pickles. How many pickles does Alice have in total?

There are <u>5 vats</u> of <u>274 pickles</u>. In maths, that's <u>5 × 274</u>.

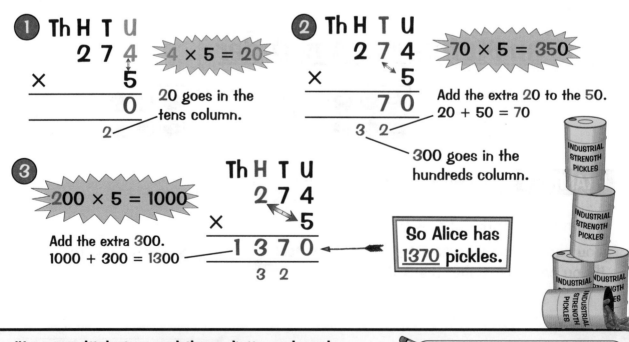

①
```
Th H T U
   2 7 4
×      5
─────────
       0
     2
```
4 × 5 = 20
20 goes in the tens column.

②
```
Th H T U
   2 7 4
×      5
─────────
     7 0
   3 2
```
70 × 5 = 350
Add the extra 20 to the 50. 20 + 50 = 70
300 goes in the hundreds column.

③
200 × 5 = 1000
```
Th H T U
   2 7 4
×      5
─────────
 1 3 7 0
   3 2
```
Add the extra 300. 1000 + 300 = 1300

So Alice has <u>1370</u> pickles.

"I can multiply two and three-digit numbers by one-digit numbers without a calculator."

Solving Calculation Problems

Problems with Addition and Subtraction

EXAMPLE: Pens cost £1.47. Gary only has 98p, so Robbie lends him £2.00.
How much money will Gary have left after he buys a pen?

First add Robbie's
money to Gary's
money...

```
u  t  h
0 . 9 8
+ 2 . 0 0
  2 . 9 8
```

...then subtract the
cost of the pen.

```
u  t  h
2 . 9 8
- 1 . 4 7
  1 . 5 1
```

So Gary will have £1.51 left.

Problems with Multiplication and Division

EXAMPLE: Jessica has invited 19 friends to a party.
How many sweets does she need so that each guest can have 8?
Work out the answer in your head.

First, work out what the question is telling you to do.
19 guests need 8 sweets each, so do 19 × 8 to find the total number of sweets.

19 × 8 is tricky in your head. But 19 is the same as 10 + 9.
So do 10 × 8 and then 9 × 8. Then add them together.

10 × 8 = 80   9 × 8 = 72   ➤   80 + 72 = 152

EXAMPLE: Anna shares 12 fish equally between her 4 pet seals.
How many fish will each seal get?

"Shared between" means "divided by". So you've got to work out 12 ÷ 4.

Use the 4 times table to find which
number gives 12 when multiplied by 4.

Dividing is the inverse
of multiplying.

Arp
Arp

```
1 × 4 = 4
2 × 4 = 8
3 × 4 = 12
4 × 4 = 16
```

Multiplying 4 by 3 gives 12.

So 12 ÷ 4 = 3.

Each seal will get 3 fish.

"I can solve problems using addition, subtraction,
multiplication and division."

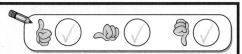

Practice Questions

Start off with the green questions — they're the easiest ones.
The blue ones are a bit harder, and the pink ones are the hardest.

1 Work out:

   a) 137 + 22   b) 782 + 441   c) 20 − 8

2 Zoë is stuck in a traffic jam. There are 22 lorries and 56 cars in front of her.

   How many vehicles are in front of Zoë in the traffic jam? 78

3 150 children went to the school disco.

   69 were boys. How many were girls?

4 643 people went to a football match in Cuckfield.
   391 people went to a football match in Newhaven.

   a) How many people went to these two football matches altogether? 1034

   b) Show how you could check your answer.

5 What is:

   a) 3 × 4?   b) 8 × 6?   c) 21 ÷ 3?

   d) 72 ÷ 8?   e) 7 × 3 × 4?   f) 10 × 8 × 2?

6 There are 42 monkeys at the zoo. Each monkey eats 3 bananas.

   How many bananas do the monkeys eat in total?

7 What is:

   a) 23 ÷ 1?

   b) 1 × 18?

   c) 794 × 0?

8 The factors of 30 are 1, 2, 3, 5, 6, 10, 15 and 30.

   Arrange the factors into factor pairs.

Practice Questions

9   Gideon says that 182 + 75 = 267.

Use inverse operations to show that Gideon is wrong.

10   Louise has 248 sweets. Her friends eat 151 of them.

    a)   Estimate how many sweets are left.

    b)   Work out how many sweets are actually left.

Do not write in this book

11   List the factors of 18.

12   Dave buys a shirt for £9.79 and a CD for £3.49. How much does he spend in total?

13   What is 796 multiplied by 8?

14   An aquarium has 360 fish.

The fish are split equally between 4 fish tanks.
How many fish are in each tank?

15   Nadia and three friends see this notice.

Nadia and her friends donate £27 each.
How much more money will the charity still need?

Please help us to save the Cumbrian Hairy Toad! We need to raise £583!

16   James buys 3 boxes of jelly beans. There are 16 flavours of jelly bean. Each box has 5 jelly beans of each flavour.

How many jelly beans has James bought in total?

17   A town has three large car parks and five small car parks. Large car parks can hold 740 cars each and small car parks can hold 144 cars each.

What is the maximum number of cars that can park in the town's car parks?

Counting in Hundredths

One Hundred Hundredths Equals One Whole

This square is divided into <u>one hundred equal parts</u>.

Each part is <u>1 hundredth</u> of the whole shape.

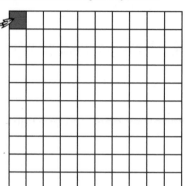

This is written as
$\frac{1}{100}$

The top number in a fraction is called the numerator. The bottom number is the denominator.

<u>100</u> of these hundredths makes <u>1 whole</u>.

Dividing Tenths by 10 Gives Hundredths

This rectangle is divided into <u>10</u> equal parts. Each part is <u>1 tenth</u>.

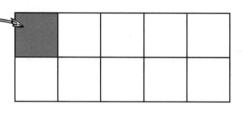

This is written as
$\frac{1}{10}$

If you <u>divide</u> each <u>tenth by ten</u>...

...the shape is then split into <u>100 equal parts</u>. Each part is <u>1 hundredth</u>.

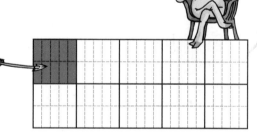

You Can Count in Hundredths

Counting in hundredths is easy. The <u>numerator</u> goes up by one each time.

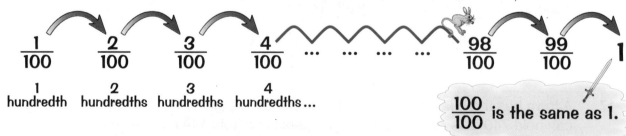

$\frac{1}{100}$ $\frac{2}{100}$ $\frac{3}{100}$ $\frac{4}{100}$ ... ... $\frac{98}{100}$ $\frac{99}{100}$ **1**

1 hundredth   2 hundredths   3 hundredths   4 hundredths...

$\frac{100}{100}$ is the same as 1.

"I know that hundredths come from dividing 1 by 100 and dividing tenths by 10. I can count in hundredths."

Equivalent Fractions

Equivalent Fractions Have the Same Value

Diagrams can help to show when fractions are <u>equivalent</u>.

EXAMPLE: $\frac{2}{3}$ and $\frac{6}{9}$ are equivalent.

Equivalent just means the fractions are <u>the same</u>, but written differently.

$\frac{2}{3}$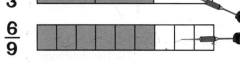

$\frac{6}{9}$

The two fractions take up the same space in the fraction bar, so they're equivalent.

EXAMPLE: $\frac{4}{16}$ and $\frac{2}{8}$ are both equivalent to <u>one quarter</u> ($\frac{1}{4}$).

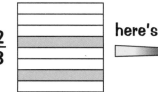 $\frac{4}{16}$ here's why 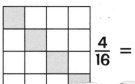 $\frac{4}{16} =$ $\frac{4}{16} =$ 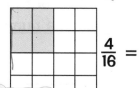 $\frac{1}{4}$

Group the shaded parts together.

$\frac{2}{8}$ here's why   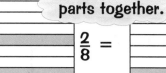 $\frac{2}{8} =$ $\frac{2}{8} =$  $\frac{1}{4}$

Spot Equivalent Fractions Using Multiples

Fractions are equivalent if you can <u>multiply</u> or <u>divide</u> the <u>numerator</u> and <u>denominator</u> of one fraction by the <u>same number</u> to get the other fraction.

EXAMPLES:

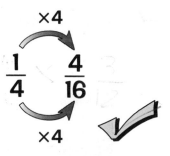

$\frac{1}{4}$ and $\frac{4}{16}$

To get from 1 to 4, you <u>multiply by 4</u>. Try multiplying 4 by 4. You get <u>16</u>, so the two fractions <u>are equivalent</u>.

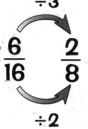

$\frac{6}{16}$ and $\frac{2}{8}$

To get from 16 to 8, you <u>divide by 2</u>. Try dividing 6 by 2. You get <u>3</u>, so the two fractions are <u>NOT equivalent</u>.

"I can show equivalent fractions using diagrams."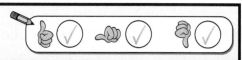

Adding and Subtracting Fractions

Adding and Subtracting Fractions

When the <u>denominators</u> of two fractions are the <u>same</u>, you can add or subtract the fractions by just using the <u>numerators</u>.

EXAMPLE: What is $\frac{4}{15} + \frac{9}{15}$?

Both denominators are the <u>same</u>.
So just <u>add the numerators</u>.

$$\frac{4}{15} + \frac{9}{15} = \frac{13}{15}$$

The bottom number needs to stay the same.

EXAMPLE: What is $\frac{11}{12} - \frac{3}{12}$?

Both denominators are the <u>same</u>.
So just <u>subtract the numerators</u>.

$$\frac{11}{12} - \frac{3}{12} = \frac{8}{12}$$

Some Fractions Add to Give More Than 1

EXAMPLE: What is $\frac{6}{9} + \frac{7}{9}$?

Add the <u>numerators</u> together. ➤

$$\frac{6}{9} + \frac{7}{9} = \frac{13}{9}$$

The numerator is <u>bigger</u> than the denominator, so the fraction is bigger than 1.
This is called an <u>improper fraction</u>.

$\frac{9}{9}$ is the <u>same as 1</u>.

This is a <u>mixed number</u>.
It's got a <u>whole number</u> part and a <u>fraction</u> part.

So subtract 9 ninths from 13 ninths to see how many ninths you're <u>left with</u>. ➤

$$\frac{13}{9} - \frac{9}{9} = \frac{4}{9}$$

So...

$$\frac{6}{9} + \frac{7}{9} = 1\frac{4}{9}$$

You can check your answer using diagrams:

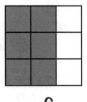 **+** **=**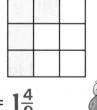

$$\frac{6}{9} \qquad \frac{7}{9} \qquad\qquad \frac{13}{9} = 1\frac{4}{9}$$

"I can add and subtract fractions."

Fractions of Amounts

Times by the Top, Divide by the Bottom

To find a fraction of any number, you always <u>divide</u> by the <u>bottom number</u> and <u>times</u> by the <u>top number</u>.

So to find $\frac{3}{8}$ of 40...

$$\frac{3}{8}$$

...you <u>multiply</u> by the numerator...

...and <u>divide</u> by the denominator.

$40 \div 8 = 5...$ ...and $5 \times 3 = \underline{15}$

It doesn't matter if you <u>multiply</u> or <u>divide</u> first. Just do what's easiest.

EXAMPLE:

Work out $\frac{6}{7}$ of 63.

This is <u>one</u> seventh of 63.

ANSWER: Divide by the denominator. ⟹ $63 \div 7 = 9$

Multiply by the numerator. ⟹ $9 \times 6 = 54$

So the answer is <u>54</u>.

EXAMPLE:

Arthur has <u>54 books</u> in his <u>library</u> and <u>48 books</u> in his <u>bedroom</u>.
He has read <u>five sixths</u> of the books in his <u>library</u>.
He has read <u>three eighths</u> of the books in his <u>bedroom</u>.
How many of his books has he read altogether?

Library: $\frac{5}{6}$ of 54 ⟹ $54 \div 6 = 9$
$9 \times 5 = 45$

Bedroom: $\frac{3}{8}$ of 48 ⟹ $48 \div 8 = 6$
$6 \times 3 = 18$

Add the two together: $45 + 18 = \underline{63\ books}$

"I can solve problems that involve calculating fractions of amounts."

Decimals

Decimals Have Tenths and Hundredths

Decimals show numbers that are <u>not whole numbers</u>.
The digits to the right of the decimal point are all <u>worth less than 1</u>.

Tens Units Tenths Hundredths

12.57

These digits have a place value smaller than 1.

Decimal point

32.1 is just a bit bigger than 32.
32.9 is almost 33.
32.5 is right in the middle between 32 and 33.

EXAMPLE: What is the value of the <u>7</u> in the number <u>5.47</u>?

The 7 is in the hundredths place. So its value is <u>7 hundredths</u> or <u>0.07</u>.

Decimals Can be Partitioned

You can <u>partition</u> decimals. It's the same thing as partitioning whole numbers.

For example...

<u>4.52</u> can be partitioned into <u>4.0</u> + <u>0.5</u> + <u>0.02</u>

<u>4 units</u>, <u>5 tenths</u> and <u>2 hundredths</u>

You Can Show Decimals on a Number Line

You can use a number line to show where decimals are.

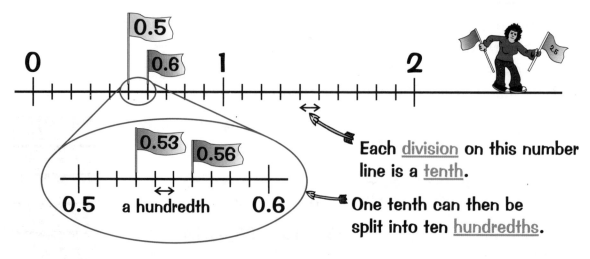

Each <u>division</u> on this number line is a <u>tenth</u>.

One tenth can then be split into ten <u>hundredths</u>.

"I can recognise decimals and understand what they show."

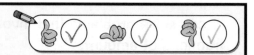

Writing Fractions as Decimals

Fractions Can be Written as Decimals

The easiest fractions to convert to decimals are <u>tenths</u> and <u>hundredths</u>.

$$\frac{1}{10} = 1 \text{ tenth} = 0.1 \qquad \frac{1}{100} = 1 \text{ hundredth} = 0.01$$

EXAMPLES: $\frac{5}{10}$ is the same as 0.5 and $\frac{3}{100}$ is the same as 0.03

BUT you can only show up to <u>9 hundredths</u> in the hundredths place.
So if you have <u>10 or more</u> hundredths, you have to put some in the tenths place.
Just remember this: <u>10 hundredths</u> are the same as <u>1 tenth</u>.

EXAMPLE: $\frac{75}{100}$ is the same as 0.75

You can't put 75 in the hundredths place. So take 70 of the hundredths and put them in the tenths place (<u>70 hundredths = 7 tenths</u>). You're just left with 5 in the hundredths place.

You can change <u>mixed numbers</u> to decimals too.

EXAMPLE: $5\frac{35}{100}$ is the same as 5.35

In this example there are 5 units and 35 hundredths. That's 5 + 0.35.

There are some others you need to know too.
<u>Learn these</u>:

$$\frac{1}{4} = 0.25 \qquad \frac{1}{2} = 0.5 \qquad \frac{3}{4} = 0.75$$

EXAMPLES: Which decimal is the same as $\frac{2}{10}$? Circle the correct answer.

2.0   20.0   (0.2)   0.02

The 2 is in the tenths place.
So the decimal represents two tenths.

Which decimal is the same as $\frac{35}{100}$?

Answer: <u>0.35</u>

The 3 is in the tenths place and the 5 is in the hundredths place.

"I can write tenths and hundredths as decimals, and ¼, ½ and ¾ as decimals."

Dividing by 10 and 100

To Divide Any Number by 10

Keep the decimal point where it is and move the digits
<u>ONE PLACE</u> to the <u>RIGHT</u> and add zeros if needed.
The number gets <u>10 times smaller</u>.

EXAMPLES:

a) $60 \div 10 = 6.0 = 6$

6.0 = 6 so you don't
need to write this zero.

The decimal point might not be shown but
it <u>always</u> comes after the <u>units place</u>.
For example, 60 is the same as 60.0

b) $82 \div 10 = 8.2$

c) $3 \div 10 = 0.3$

You need to add a zero in here
to fill the gap that's been left
before the decimal place.

To Divide Any Number by 100

Keep the decimal point where it is and move the digits
<u>TWO PLACES</u> to the <u>RIGHT</u> and add zeros if needed.
The number gets <u>100 times smaller</u>.

EXAMPLES:

a) $70 \div 100 = 0.70 = 0.7$

b) $2 \div 100 = 0.02$

c) $83 \div 100 = 0.83$

Remember to <u>remove unnecessary</u>
zeros at the end, e.g. you can
write 0.70 as just 0.7

<u>AND</u> there has to be a digit
to the left of the decimal
point, so you'd have to put
0.7 instead of .7

"I can divide a one or two-digit number by 10 or 100."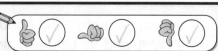

Rounding Decimals

1 d.p. is One Number After the Decimal Point

A number with <u>one decimal place</u> (d.p.) has <u>one number</u> after the decimal point.

EXAMPLES:

23.6   1.3   99.9
18.9   9.4   0.7

Sometimes you want a <u>whole number</u> though (one without any decimal places).
So you can <u>round</u> a decimal to the <u>nearest whole number</u>.

Rounding Decimals

Rounding to a whole number is easy as long as you remember the <u>rules</u>:

Rounding to a Whole Number

1) The number always lies <u>between two possible answers</u>.
   You have to decide which one it's <u>nearest to</u>.

2) Look at the digit to the <u>right</u> of the decimal point.

3) If the number is <u>5 or more</u> then <u>round UP</u>.
   If the number is <u>less than 5</u> then <u>round DOWN</u>.

EXAMPLES:

Round <u>17.3</u> to the nearest whole number.

The number lies between <u>17</u> and <u>18</u>.
The number after the decimal point is 3.
So <u>round DOWN</u> to <u>17</u>.

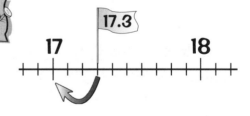

Round <u>12.5</u> to the nearest whole number.

The number lies between <u>12</u> and <u>13</u>.
The number after the decimal point is 5.
So <u>round UP</u> to <u>13</u>.

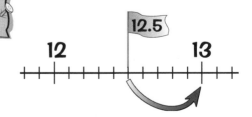

"I can round decimals with one decimal place
to the nearest whole number."

Comparing Decimals

Ascending order means from lowest to highest.
Descending order means from highest to lowest.

Decimals Can be Put in Ascending Order...

EXAMPLE: Put these in ascending order: 6.5   5.2   11.4   11.3   10.9

First look at the <u>whole</u> numbers
(to the left of the decimal point).
Put them in ascending order:
5 first, then 6, then 10, then 11.

5.2   6.5   10.9   11.4   11.3

Then look at the <u>decimal places</u>.
11.3 is smaller than 11.4 so put it first.

5.2   6.5   10.9   (11.3   11.4)

So the right order is <u>5.2, 6.5, 10.9, 11.3, 11.4</u>

...or in Descending Order

EXAMPLE: Put these in <u>descending order</u>: 12.51   1.34   2.31   2.34   2.43

First look at the <u>whole</u> numbers
(to the left of the decimal point).
Put them in descending order:
12 first, then 2, then 1.

12.51   2.31   2.34   2.43   1.34

Then look at the <u>first decimal
places</u>. 2.43 is bigger than
2.31 or 2.34 so put it first.
(2.31 and 2.34 both have 3 tenths.)

12.51 (2.43   2.31   2.34) 1.34

Now order 2.31 and 2.34.
Look at their <u>second decimal places</u>.
2.34 is bigger so it goes first.

12.51   2.43 (2.34   2.31) 1.34

So the right order is <u>12.51, 2.43, 2.34, 2.31, 1.34</u>

"I can compare numbers with the same number
of decimal places."

Solving Fraction and Decimal Problems

Measurements Can be Given in Decimals

Bob has built a new house. Its width is <u>12.2 metres</u>.
He builds a model of his house that is <u>ten times smaller</u>.
How wide is his <u>model</u>?

It's ten times smaller, so <u>divide by 10</u>. 12.2 m ÷ 10 = <u>1.22 metres</u>
Move each digit one place to the right.

You Can Solve Some Problems in Two Ways

EXAMPLE:

Anna has £77. She gives $\frac{5}{7}$ of it to charity. How much is left?

There are <u>two ways</u> to do this. You get the <u>same answer</u> either way.

1 Work out how much money $\frac{5}{7}$ of £77 is, and then <u>subtract</u> this from £77.

$$£77 ÷ 7 = £11 \qquad £11 × 5 = £55$$

$$£77 - £55 = £22$$

So she has <u>£22</u> left.

2 Work out what <u>fraction</u> she <u>keeps</u>, and find this as a fraction of £77.

Anna gives $\frac{5}{7}$ to charity.

Subtract this from $\frac{7}{7}$ to find out how much she <u>keeps</u>.

$\frac{7}{7}$ is the same as 1. $\frac{7}{7} - \frac{5}{7} = \frac{2}{7}$ So Anna keeps $\frac{2}{7}$ of the £77.

Then work out what $\frac{2}{7}$ of £77 is:

$$£77 ÷ 7 = £11 \quad £11 × 2 = £22$$

So she has <u>£22</u> left.

"I can solve measure and money problems that
involve fractions and decimals."

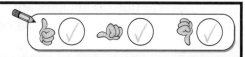

Practice Questions

Start off with the **green** questions — they're the easiest ones.
The **blue** ones are a bit harder, and the **pink** ones are the hardest.

1   Here is part of a number line.

What number is the arrow pointing to?

2   Work out:

   a) $\frac{5}{11} + \frac{3}{11}$ b) $\frac{11}{16} + \frac{2}{16}$ c) $\frac{3}{25} + \frac{16}{25}$

3   Work out:

   a) $\frac{9}{10} - \frac{3}{10}$ b) $\frac{8}{17} - \frac{5}{17}$ c) $\frac{19}{21} - \frac{11}{21}$

4   Put the following decimals in order. Start with the smallest.

         12.8   11.2   11.8   12.1   11.6   12.0

5   Round the following decimals to the nearest whole number.

   a)   9.6   b)   8.9   c)   16.5   d)   128.2

6   Write the following fractions as decimals.

   a) $\frac{8}{10}$ b) $\frac{98}{100}$ c) $\frac{3}{4}$

7   Circle the fraction that is equivalent to $\frac{2}{6}$.

         $\frac{4}{16}$ $\frac{6}{18}$ $\frac{1}{12}$ $\frac{3}{24}$

8   Jim has a sheet of 90 stickers. He gives 10 to each of his friends.

   He has no stickers left.
   How many people did he give stickers to?

Practice Questions

9   A fraction of the circle below has been shaded in.
     Shade in the equivalent amount of the square.

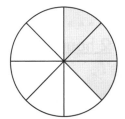 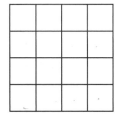

10   Work out the following calculations. Give each answer as a mixed number.

a) $\frac{5}{7} + \frac{4}{7}$ b) $\frac{11}{15} + \frac{9}{15}$ c) $\frac{6}{20} + \frac{19}{20}$

11   Tim is thinking of a decimal.
     He says: "It is bigger than 11 and smaller than 12. It has one
     decimal place. It rounds to 11 to the nearest whole number."

     Give the possible decimals that Tim could be thinking of.

12   Find the numbers that should go in the boxes below.

a) $\frac{4}{\square} = \frac{32}{40}$ b) $\frac{2}{5} = \frac{14}{\square}$

13   A plant is 122 cm tall. Another plant is ten times shorter. How tall is this plant?

     Give your answer to the nearest whole number.

14   Gerald grew 72 tomatoes. He ate $\frac{4}{9}$ of them and gave $\frac{2}{9}$ of them to his friend.

     How many tomatoes are left?

15   Abby and Rick each have a cake. Abby eats $\frac{6}{7}$ of her cake. Rick eats $\frac{3}{7}$ of his cake.

     How much cake is left over altogether? Give your answer as a fraction.

Units

Sometimes You Need to Convert Units

Converting units just means changing from one set of units to another.

EXAMPLES:

Sheila's train journey took <u>2 hours</u> and <u>5 minutes</u>.
How long is this in <u>minutes</u>?

1 hour = 60 minutes

Here you're converting from hours to minutes.

2 hours = 2 × 60 minutes = 120 minutes.
So it's 120 minutes + 5 minutes = <u>125 minutes</u>.

Larry has run <u>1.5 km</u>. Kyle ran <u>300 metres</u> further.
How far did Kyle run in <u>metres</u>?

1 km = 1000 m

You need to give your answer in metres, so convert all the units into metres.

1.5 km = 1.5 × 1000 m = 1500 m.
So Kyle ran 1500 m + 300 m = <u>1800 m</u>.

You Can Compare Values with the Same Units

It's easier to <u>compare</u> measurements when they're in the <u>same units</u>.

EXAMPLE: <u>Fish bowl A</u> has a capacity of <u>7.8 l</u>. <u>Fish bowl B</u> has a capacity of <u>7500 ml</u>. Which bowl can hold more water?

Put both capacities into the <u>same units</u>.

| 1 litre = 1000 ml |

So to convert l to ml, <u>multiply by 1000</u>.

Fish bowl A's capacity = 7.8 × 1000 = 7800 ml

7800 ml is <u>more</u> than 7500 ml. So <u>Fish bowl A</u> can hold more water.

"I can convert between units and compare measurements."

Perimeter

Finding the Perimeter of a Shape

Perimeter is the distance <u>all the way around the outside</u> of a 2D (flat) shape.

To find the perimeter, put a <u>cross</u> at one vertex, then go around the shape <u>adding up</u> the lengths of all the sides. When you get back to the cross, <u>stop</u>.

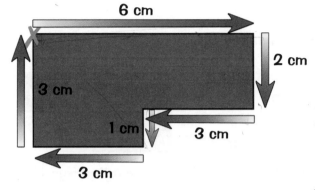

6 cm
2 cm
3 cm
1 cm
3 cm
3 cm

A vertex is a corner.

Perimeter = 6 + 2 + 3 + 1 + 3 + 3
= <u>18 cm</u>

Perimeters of Squares and Rectangles

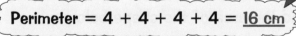

You can work out the perimeter of a <u>square</u> from the length of just <u>one side</u>.

EXAMPLE: Calculate the perimeter of the <u>square</u>.

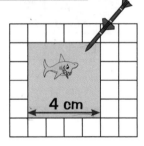

4 cm

All the sides of a square are the <u>same length</u>. So, you can write the other lengths on...
...and then work out the perimeter.

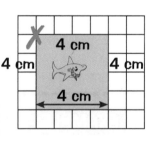

4 cm
4 cm
4 cm
4 cm

Perimeter = 4 + 4 + 4 + 4 = <u>16 cm</u>

This is the same as 4 × 4 = <u>16 cm</u>.

You can work out the perimeter of a <u>rectangle</u> from <u>two lengths</u>.

EXAMPLE: Find the perimeter of the <u>rectangle</u>.

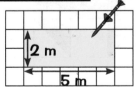

2 m
5 m

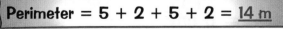

<u>Opposite</u> sides of a rectangle are the <u>same length</u>. So...

5 m
2 m
2 m
5 m

Perimeter = 5 + 2 + 5 + 2 = <u>14 m</u>

This is the same as (5 + 2) × 2 = <u>14 m</u>.

"I can work out the perimeters of shapes."

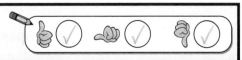

Area

You Can Find Area by Counting Squares

This square has 1 cm sides.
It is called a <u>square centimetre</u>.
The short way to write this is <u>cm^2</u>.

I've got one. Leg it!

The <u>area</u> of a shape is the amount of <u>space</u> it takes up.

It's easy to work out the area of a shape. Just <u>count</u>
the <u>number</u> of <u>square centimetres</u> it takes up.

> <u>Mark or number the squares</u> as you count.
> That way you'll only count each square <u>once</u>.

1	2	3	4
5	6	7	

<u>7 square centimetres</u> (7 cm^2)

EXAMPLE: Find the area of this yellow shape.

Each square is a square centimetre.
So <u>count the yellow squares</u>.

The area of the shape is <u>10 cm^2</u>.

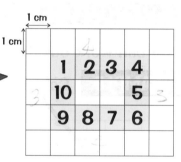

1 cm

1 cm

	1	2	3	4	
	10			5	
	9	8	7	6	

EXAMPLE: Find the area of the shape below.

1. Count the number of <u>whole squares</u>.
   There are 4 whole squares = 4 cm^2.

2. The shape also covers <u>2 half squares</u>.
   So the area covered by the half squares is
   $$\frac{1}{2}\,cm^2 + \frac{1}{2}\,cm^2 = 1\,cm^2$$

3. So the total area of the shape is
   $$4\,cm^2 + 1\,cm^2 = \underline{5\,cm^2}$$

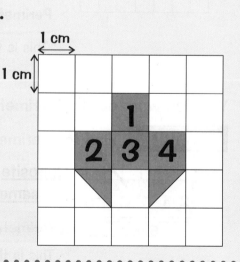

1 cm

1 cm

"I can find the areas of shapes by counting squares."

Money

Decimals are Used for Money

Decimals are used for <u>money</u>. Pence are <u>hundredths</u> of a pound. So...

> £1.23 is £1 and 23p   £1.05 is £1 and 5p   £1.50 is £1 and 50p

<u>Money</u> is always written with <u>two decimal places</u>, even if there are just 0s on the end. You write £1.50, not £1.5.

Lots of Calculations Involve Money

EXAMPLE: Richard buys a lolly that costs 85p and a drink that costs 40p. How much change does he get from £5?

First, find out how much Richard <u>spends</u> in total.   **85 + 40 = 125**   Richard spends 125p or £1.25.

Then find out how much <u>change</u> he gets. £5 means £5.00, so...

£5.00 – £1.25

$$
\begin{array}{r}
4\ \overset{9}{\cancel{10}}\\
5\ .\ \overset{10}{\cancel{0}}\ {}^{1}0\\
-\ 1\ .\ 2\ 5\\
\hline
3\ .\ 7\ 5
\end{array}
$$

Richard gets £3.75 change.

Sometimes you might find it easier to <u>convert</u> from <u>pounds</u> to <u>pence</u> when you're doing a calculation with money.

EXAMPLE: Apples cost <u>90p per kg</u>. Kate buys <u>2 kg of apples</u>. How much <u>change</u> will she get from <u>£5</u>?

Work out how much Kate <u>spends</u>: 90p + 90p = 180p

Convert the £5 to pence: £5.00 = 500p

Work out how much <u>change</u> Kate gets: 500p – 180p = 320p

Convert the answer back into pounds: 320p = <u>£3.20</u>.

"I can do calculations involving money, in pounds and pence."

Clocks

Analogue Clocks are the Ones with Hands

The little hand tells you the hour and the big hand tells you the minutes.

5 minutes past 12

10 minutes past 12

15 minutes past 12

> Each time the big hand goes from one number to the next, 5 minutes have passed.

After thirty minutes you say "minutes to" because it's closer to the next hour.

So you'd say 25 minutes to 3 instead of 35 minutes past 2.

15 minutes past = "quarter past"
30 minutes past = "half past"
15 minutes to = "quarter to"

Digital Clocks just have Numbers

Digital clocks are easy to read. You just say one number after the other.

EXAMPLE: This clock shows two-thirty. This number is the hour...

"Two-thirty" and "half past two" both mean 30 minutes past 2.

...and this is how many minutes past the hour.

Time can be in the 12-hour or 24-hour Clock

The 12-hour clock uses 'am' and 'pm'. 'am' means morning — it runs from 12 midnight to 12 noon (midday). 'pm' means afternoon and evening — it runs from 12 noon to 12 midnight.

The 24-hour clock is the same as the 12-hour clock in the morning. In the afternoon, you need to add 12 hours on to the 12-hour clock to find the time in the 24-hour clock.

So...

Ten past two in the morning: 2:10 am in the 12-hour clock, 02:10 in the 24-hour clock.

Ten past two in the afternoon: 2:10 pm in the 12-hour clock, 14:10 in the 24-hour clock.

"I can read and write time in the 12 and 24-hour clock, and can convert between analogue and digital."

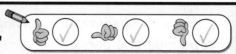

Time Problems

There are Lots of Units For Time

Time can be measured in <u>seconds</u>, <u>minutes</u> or <u>hours</u>.

 60 seconds = 1 minute   60 minutes = 1 hour   24 hours = 1 day

It can also be measured in <u>days</u>, <u>weeks</u>, <u>months</u> and <u>years</u>.

7 days = 1 week   12 months = 1 year

You Can Solve Problems By Changing Units

EXAMPLE: Jason got on the bus at <u>9:20</u>. He got off again at <u>10:40</u>. How long was the bus ride <u>in hours and minutes</u>?

Break the time up into <u>simple steps</u>.

9:20 ⟶ 10:00 ⟶ 10:40
+40 mins   +40 mins

40 mins + 40 mins = **80 minutes**

Now change it to <u>hours and minutes</u>. There are 60 minutes in an hour.

80 minutes = 60 minutes + 20 minutes
= 1 hour + 20 minutes

So the journey took <u>1 hour and 20 minutes</u>.

EXAMPLE: Sofia is <u>two years and six months</u> old. How old is she in <u>months</u>?

Change 2 years into <u>months</u>.

1 year = 12 months
So 2 years = 12 × 2 = 24 months

<u>Add on</u> the 6 months.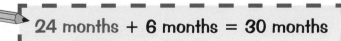

24 months + 6 months = 30 months

So Sophia is <u>30 months old</u>.

"I can solve problems by changing between different units of time."

Practice Questions

Start off with the green questions — they're the easiest ones.
The blue ones are a bit harder, and the pink ones are the hardest.

1   Change these measurements:

   a)   3 kilometres into metres.

   b)   4 hours and 12 minutes into minutes.

   c)   3 minutes to seconds.

Do not write in this book

2   Which measurement is bigger:

   a)   120 minutes or 2 hours and 10 minutes?

   b)   £3 or 260p?

   c)   1500 m or 1.8 km?

3   Find the perimeter of this shape.

   Not drawn to scale.

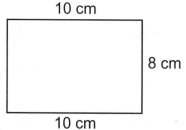

10 cm

8 cm   8 cm

10 cm

4   What is the area of the shape on the grid?

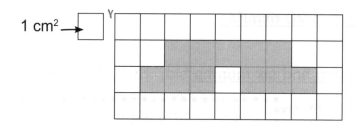

1 cm²

5   Change the prices below from pounds to pence.

   a)   £2.99   b)   £3.75   c)   £0.25   d)   £0.05

6   What is...

   a)   3.45 pm in the 24-hour clock?   b)   07.20 in the 12-hour clock?

   c)   16:30 in the 12-hour clock?   d)   8:12 am in the 24-hour clock?

Practice Questions

7   Some prices at a shop are shown on the right.

Adam buys 1 packet of crisps, 1 drink
and 2 chocolate bars.

How much does he spend?

> Drinks: £1.25
> Crisps: 80p
> Chocolate: 75p

8   Find the perimeter of the square and rectangle below.

a)

5 cm

square

Not drawn
to scale.

b)

9 cm

4.5 cm   rectangle

Not drawn to scale.

9   What time do the clocks below show? Give your answer in the 12-hour clock.

a)

morning

b)

evening

c)

  22:35

10   Aisha has been living in her house for 1.5 years. How many months is this?

11   Jared started work at 9 am. He finished work at 5:30 pm.
He had a 1 hour lunch break.

How long did he spend working? Give your answer in hours and minutes.

12   Milly buys a magazine that costs £2.25, a tea that's 65p and a scone that costs
£2.20. She pays with a £10 note. How much change should she get?

13   Look at the shape on the grid.

a)   What is the perimeter
of the shape?

b)   What is the area of the shape?

1 cm

1 cm

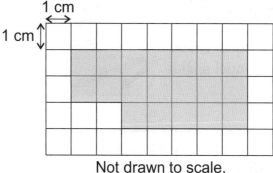

Not drawn to scale.

Comparing 2D Shapes

Polygons have Straight Sides

The <u>name</u> of a polygon tells you <u>how many sides and angles</u> it has.

<u>tri</u>angle	<u>quad</u>rilateral	<u>penta</u>gon	<u>hexa</u>gon	<u>hepta</u>gon	<u>octa</u>gon
3 sides	4 sides	5 sides	6 sides	7 sides	8 sides
3 angles	4 angles	5 angles	6 angles	7 angles	8 angles

Regular Polygons have Equal Length Sides

<u>Regular polygons</u> have <u>equal length sides</u> and <u>equal angles</u>.
<u>Irregular polygons</u> have at least one <u>side</u> or <u>angle</u> that's <u>different</u>.

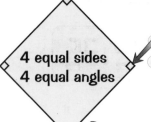

4 equal sides
4 equal angles

Each angle is a right angle (90°). It's just a quarter of a turn.

2 pairs of equal sides

<u>Squares</u> are
regular polygons.

<u>Rectangles</u> are
irregular polygons.

<u>An irregular</u>
<u>hexa</u>gon

There are Different Types of Triangle

AN EQUILATERAL
TRIANGLE

3 equal sides
3 equal angles

60°

Each angle in
an equilateral
triangle is 60°.

60°   60°

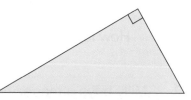

A RIGHT-ANGLED TRIANGLE
1 angle is a <u>right angle</u>.

AN ISOSCELES
TRIANGLE

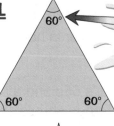

2 equal sides
2 equal angles

A SCALENE TRIANGLE
<u>All</u> the sides and
angles are <u>different</u>.

"I can identify 2D shapes, including quadrilaterals
and triangles."

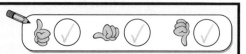

Comparing 2D Shapes

There's More to Quadrilaterals than Squares...

Quadrilaterals are 2D shapes with 4 sides.

SQUARE

4 equal sides.
Diagonals meet
at right angles.

4 right angles.
2 pairs of parallel sides.

RECTANGLE

2 pairs of equal sides.

These sides are perpendicular.

RHOMBUS

4 sides of
equal length.

Opposite sides
are parallel.
Opposite angles
are equal.

PARALLELOGRAM

Opposite
sides are the
same length.

TRAPEZIUM

1 pair of
parallel
sides.

KITE

Two pairs of equal
length sides.
No sides are parallel.

What Shape Am I?

You can work out what a shape is from information about its sides and angles.

EXAMPLES:

"I have 3 sides and
2 equal angles."

"I am an isosceles
triangle."

"I have 4 equal sides
and all my angles
are right angles."

"I am a
square."

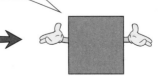

"I can identify 2D shapes, including quadrilaterals
and triangles."

Comparing Angles

An Angle is a Measure of Turn

Angles tell you <u>how much something has turned</u>.
Angles are measured in <u>degrees (°)</u>.

No, I said an <u>angle</u>.

There are 90°
in a $\frac{1}{4}$ turn...   ...180° in a $\frac{1}{2}$ turn   ...and 360°
in a full turn.

Angles are given different <u>names</u>
according to how <u>big</u> they are:

Remember, you
use a <u>square</u> to
show a right angle.

If it's <u>between</u> a $\frac{1}{4}$
and $\frac{1}{2}$ turn, then it's
an <u>OBTUSE</u> angle.

If it's <u>less than</u> a
$\frac{1}{4}$ turn, then it's
an <u>ACUTE</u> angle.

If it's <u>exactly</u> a $\frac{1}{4}$ turn,
then it's a <u>RIGHT</u> angle.

EXAMPLES:

These are smaller than a $\frac{1}{4}$
turn, so they are <u>ACUTE</u>.

These are bigger than right
angles so they are <u>OBTUSE</u>.

Comparing Angles by Size

You can <u>order angles</u> by their <u>size</u>.

EXAMPLE:

Look at these <u>angles</u>. Put them in
<u>order of size</u> from <u>smallest</u> to <u>largest</u>.

This is an
acute angle.

This is a
right angle.

This is an
obtuse angle.

This is an even bigger
obtuse angle.

SMALLEST

LARGEST

"I can identify acute and obtuse angles. I can
compare angles and put them in order of size."

Finding Lines of Symmetry

Some Shapes have Reflective Symmetry

This shape has a <u>mirror line</u>. It is also called the <u>line of symmetry</u>.

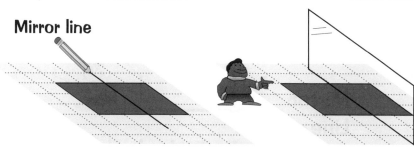

Mirror line

Bob looks in the mirror. It looks as if he can see the <u>whole shape</u>.

If you can draw <u>two</u> mirror lines you say there are <u>two</u> lines of symmetry.
If you can draw <u>three</u> there are <u>three</u> lines of symmetry.
And so on...
If you can't draw <u>any</u> there are <u>no</u> lines of symmetry.

1 LINE OF SYMMETRY

2 LINES OF SYMMETRY

3 LINES OF SYMMETRY

NO LINES OF SYMMETRY

NO LINES OF SYMMETRY

EXAMPLE: Is this shape <u>symmetrical</u>? If it is, draw in its <u>lines of symmetry</u>.

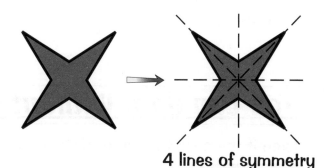

4 lines of symmetry

EXAMPLE: Shade in more squares to make a <u>symmetrical pattern</u>.

The shading must be the same on both sides of the mirror line.

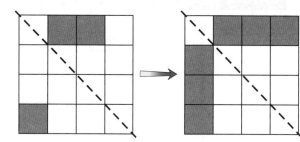

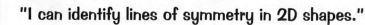

"I can identify lines of symmetry in 2D shapes."

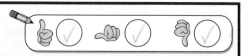

Completing Symmetrical Shapes

Reflecting Shapes in a Mirror Line

You need to be able to <u>reflect a shape</u> in its <u>mirror line</u>.

EXAMPLE:

Draw the <u>reflection</u> of this shape in the mirror line.

Mirror
Line

ANSWER:

This vertex is 2 squares from the mirror line.

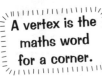

A vertex is the maths word for a corner.

So the reflected vertex must be 2 squares away.

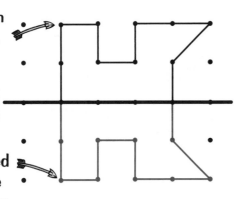

1) <u>Reflect</u> the vertices <u>one at a time</u>.
   - Count the squares <u>between</u> the vertex and the mirror line.
   - Count the <u>same</u> number of squares on the other side of the mirror line.
   - Draw the <u>reflected</u> vertex.

2) Join up your reflected vertices with <u>straight</u> lines.

You Can do it Without Points

Even if there isn't a grid of dots, you can still draw a reflection.

EXAMPLE: Reflect the shape below in the mirror line.

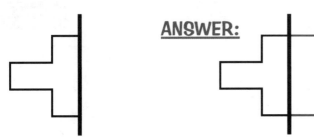

ANSWER:

You just need to reflect each line one at a time. Measure each line with a ruler or use tracing paper.

"I can complete a symmetrical shape."

Coordinates

Go Across then Up to Find the Position

Each point on a grid has <u>two</u> numbers to show its position.
These are called <u>coordinates</u>.

Coordinates tell you how many across and how many up from 0 a point is. You find them using the x-axis and y-axis.

<u>The y-axis is a vertical line on the left</u> of the grid.

<u>The x-axis is a horizontal line across</u> the bottom of the grid.

Gary

Coordinates are always put in <u>brackets</u> like this: (1, 4).
(0, 0) is called the <u>origin</u>.

EXAMPLE: Gary's coordinates are: **(3, 2)**

The x-coordinate tells you how many <u>across</u>.

The y-coordinate tells you how many <u>up</u>.

X Goes Before Y

You <u>always</u> put the x-coordinate <u>before</u> the y-coordinate.
Here are some handy ways to remember it:

1. The two coordinates are in <u>alphabetical order</u> — x then y.
2. The x axis goes <u>across</u> the page.
   In other words "<u>x is a...cross</u>", get it? — x is a "✗".
3. You always go <u>in the house</u> (→) and then
   <u>up the stairs</u> (↑), so it's <u>along</u> first and then <u>up</u>.

"I can describe a position on a grid as coordinates."

Translations

Translation _is_ Sliding

A <u>translation</u> is where a shape <u>slides</u> from one place to another, <u>without rotating</u> or <u>flipping over</u>.

EXAMPLES:

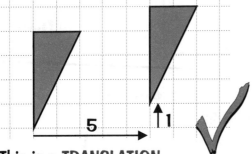

5

1

This is a <u>TRANSLATION</u>.
The triangle has moved <u>5 squares</u> to the <u>right</u> and <u>1 square up</u>.

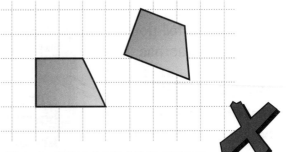

This is <u>NOT A TRANSLATION</u>.
The shape has <u>turned</u> as well as sliding.

Count Squares _to Describe Translations_

To <u>describe</u> a translation you need to say how many squares <u>left</u> or <u>right</u> the shape has moved and how many squares <u>up</u> or <u>down</u> it's moved.

EXAMPLES:

You need to...

1. Pick a <u>corner</u>.

2. <u>Count</u> how many squares <u>left</u> or <u>right</u> it's moved.

3. <u>Count</u> how many squares <u>up</u> or <u>down</u> it's moved.

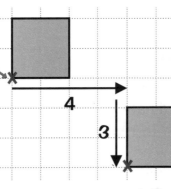

4

3

This square has been translated <u>4 squares right</u> and <u>3 squares down</u>.

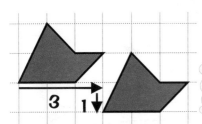

3   1

This shape has been translated <u>3 squares right</u> and <u>1 square down</u>.

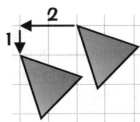

2

1

This shape has been translated <u>2 squares left</u> and <u>1 square down</u>.

"I can describe translations."

Drawing Shapes on Grids

You Can Draw Shapes on a Grid

EXAMPLE:

Plot the following points:

(1,1) (4,1) (6,4) (2,4)

What shape do you get if you join the points?

ANSWER: Trapezium

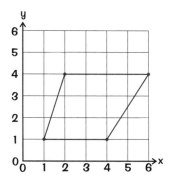

You Can Use Coordinates to Complete Shapes

EXAMPLE:

A, B and C are three vertices of a rectangle. Write the coordinates of the fourth vertex.

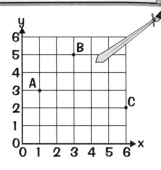

Two sides of the rectangle can be drawn in straight away.

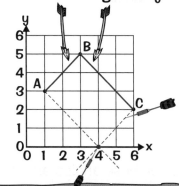

Draw in lines parallel to these, starting from points A and C.

The fourth vertex is where they meet. Its coordinates are (4, 0).

EXAMPLE:

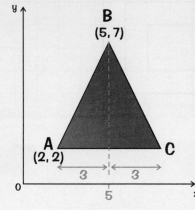

This is an isosceles triangle. Sides AB and BC are the same length. Find the coordinates of point C.

Point C is straight across from point A, so it must have the same y-coordinate as A. That's 2.

It's an isosceles triangle so it's symmetrical.
So B must be halfway across the triangle.
The difference between the x-coordinates of
A and B = 5 – 2 = 3.
So point C must have the x-coordinate 5 + 3 = 8.

So C's coordinates must be (8, 2).

"I can plot coordinates and draw sides to complete shapes."

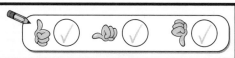

Practice Questions

Start off with the **green** questions — they're the easiest ones.
The **blue** ones are a bit harder, and the **pink** ones are the hardest.

1   A shape has 2 pairs of equal length sides. None of the sides are parallel.

What type of quadrilateral is it?

2   Which of these triangles are isosceles?

3   Look at these angles.

a)   Put these angles in order of size from smallest to largest.

b)   Which of these angles are obtuse?

4   Copy the grids below.

Draw lines to complete the shapes so that they are symmetrical in the mirror line.

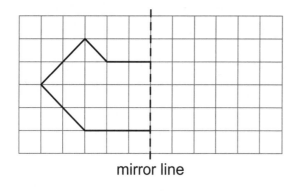

mirror line

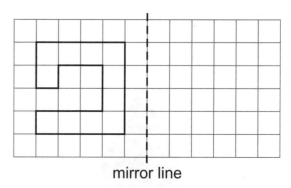

mirror line

5   Copy the grid below.

Shade in more squares to
make a symmetrical pattern.

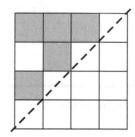

Practice Questions

6 Which of these shapes have more than one line of symmetry?

A 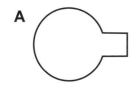   B   C   D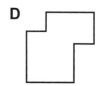

7 A map has been drawn on this grid.

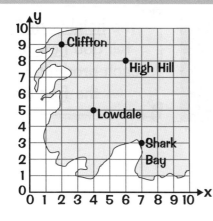

a) Write the coordinates of Shark Bay.

b) Write the coordinates of High Hill.

8 Shape B is a translation of Shape A.
Describe the translation.

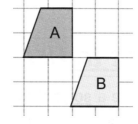

9 Point B on this triangle has coordinates (1, 2).
The triangle is translated 3 squares to the right.
What are the coordinates of point B now?

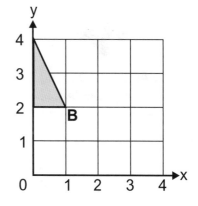

10 A, B and C are three vertices of a parallelogram.
Their coordinates are: **A** (3, 2) **B** (2, 0) **C** (0, 3).

a) Copy this grid. Plot A, B and C on your grid.

b) Work out the coordinates of the fourth vertex.

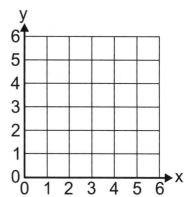

Bar Charts

Bar Charts Show Data using Heights of Bars

A <u>bar chart</u> is a way of showing data so it's <u>clear</u> and easy to understand.
They help you <u>compare</u> data without having to look at lots of numbers.

<u>Vertical axis</u>
with <u>labels</u>

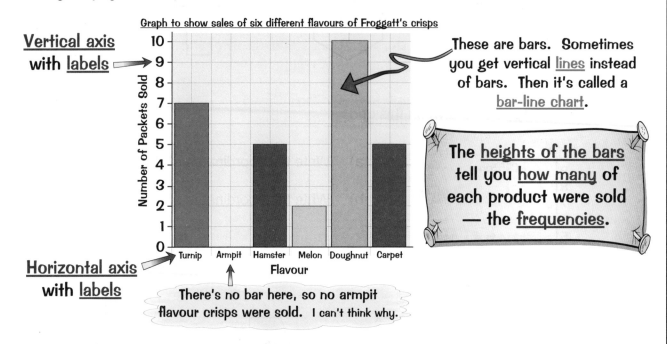

Graph to show sales of six different flavours of Froggatt's crisps

These are bars. Sometimes
you get vertical <u>lines</u> instead
of bars. Then it's called a
<u>bar-line chart</u>.

The <u>heights of the bars</u>
tell you <u>how many</u> of
each product were sold
— the <u>frequencies</u>.

<u>Horizontal axis</u>
with <u>labels</u>

There's no bar here, so no armpit
flavour crisps were sold. I can't think why.

It's Important to Use the Right Scale

Bar charts need to have a <u>scale</u> that makes the data <u>easy to understand</u>.
These two bar charts show the <u>same</u> data but have <u>different</u> scales.

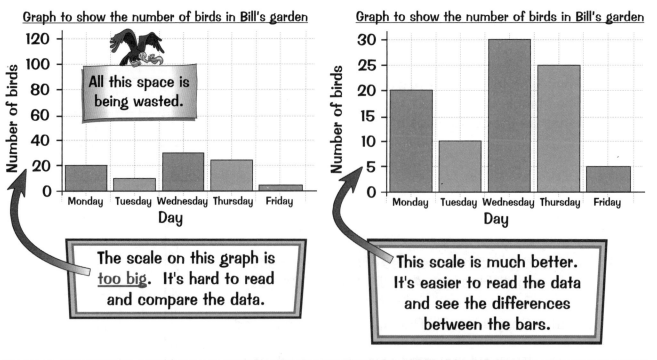

All this space is
being wasted.

The scale on this graph is
<u>too big</u>. It's hard to read
and compare the data.

This scale is much better.
It's easier to read the data
and see the differences
between the bars.

"I can interpret and present data using bar charts."

Time Graphs

Some Things Change Over Time

Time graphs are a good way to show things that change over time — like distance or temperature.

Time	Speed
30 s	20 mph
60 s	75 mph
90 s	68 mph
120 s	33 mph

EXAMPLE: The table shows the speed of Zan the Genie at different times during an egg and spoon race. Plot the speeds on a time graph.

Step 1

Write a TITLE. Then draw and label the AXES.

Then number the axes. Go up in equal jumps (don't just put on the numbers from the table). And make sure that the biggest numbers in the table will fit on.

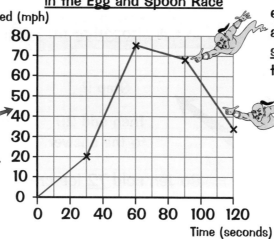

Graph to Show Zan's Speed in the Egg and Spoon Race

Step 2

Now draw a CROSS for each point. Find the time along the bottom and the speed up the side. Draw the cross where they meet.

Step 3

Then join the crosses with LINES. You don't know how Zan's speed changed between the crosses. So it's best to use STRAIGHT lines.

You Can Find Information From Graphs

EXAMPLE:

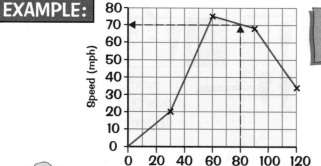

a) How fast was Zan going at 80 seconds?

Find 80 seconds on the horizontal axis and go straight up to the red line.

Now look left to the vertical axis and read the value from there.

His speed was 70 mph.

b) How much did Zan's speed increase by between 30 seconds and 60 seconds?

Read Zan's speed at 30 seconds and 60 seconds off the graph.
        (20 mph)   (75 mph)

Then, subtract his speed at 30 seconds from his speed at 60 seconds.

75 mph – 20 mph = 55 mph.

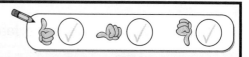

"I can interpret and present data on time graphs."

Interpreting Charts and Graphs

Some Problems Use Tables...

EXAMPLE: Jen sells ice creams in three flavours.
The table shows how many of each flavour she sold on three days.

	Friday	Saturday	Sunday
Cheese	16	18	11
Potato	18	25	20
Onion	17	29	15

How many ice creams did Jen sell altogether on Saturday?

Step 1

First add 18 and 25.

```
 T U
 1 8
+2 5
 4 3
 1
```

Step 2

Then add 29 to the answer.

```
 T U
 4 3
+2 9
 7 2
 1
```

So Jen sold **72** ice creams altogether.

...and Others Use Pictograms

Pictograms are charts that use <u>pictures</u>. This one shows how many cheese flavour ice creams Jen sold.

The <u>key</u> shows what the pictures mean.

Friday	🍦🍦🍦🍦🍦🍦🍦🍦
Saturday	🍦🍦🍦🍦🍦🍦🍦🍦🍦
Sunday	🍦🍦🍦🍦🍦½

Key 🍦 = 2 ice creams

For example, this row shows <u>9 × 2</u> ice creams = <u>18 ice creams</u>

A full picture means 2 ice creams, so <u>half</u> a picture means <u>1</u>.

How many cheese flavour ice creams did Jen sell on Friday and Saturday?

There are <u>8 full pictures</u> for Friday, so Jen sold 8 × 2 = <u>16 ice creams</u>.
There are <u>9 full pictures</u> for Saturday, so Jen sold 9 × 2 = <u>18 ice creams</u>.

In total, Jen sold 16 + 18 = <u>34 ice creams</u> on Friday and Saturday.

"I can solve problems using tables and pictograms."

Interpreting Charts and Graphs

Charts Can Be Used To Compare Data

EXAMPLE: The bar chart shows how many coloured cacti Brian is growing.

 Does Brian have more pink cacti or purple cacti?

Graph to show the number of coloured cacti Brian is growing

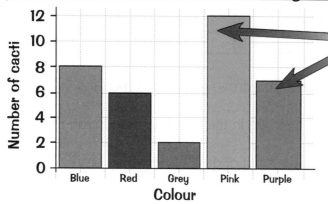

 The bar for pink cacti is <u>taller</u> than the bar for purple cacti.

So Brian has <u>more pink cacti</u>.

 How many more blue cacti does Brian have than red cacti?

Number of blue cacti = 8   Number of red cacti = 6

8 – 6 = 2 — Brian has <u>2 more</u> blue cacti than red cacti.

You Can Work Out Length of Time from Graphs

Robin cycled from Manchester to Sheffield. Use the graph to work out <u>how long</u> he was more than <u>400 metres</u> above sea level.

Find 400 metres on the <u>vertical axis</u> and draw a line across.

Then you can see when Robin was <u>above</u> 400 metres.

He went above 400 m at 3 hours...   ...and back below 400 m at 5 hours.

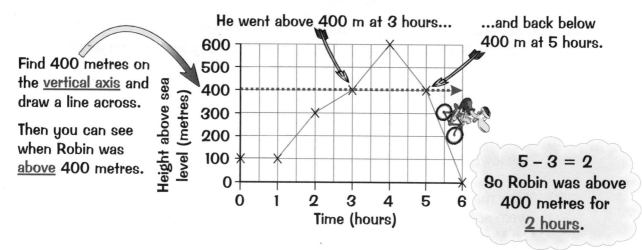

5 – 3 = 2
So Robin was above 400 metres for <u>2 hours</u>.

"I can solve problems and make comparisons using data from bar charts and time graphs."

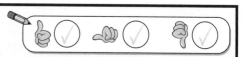

Practice Questions

Start off with the green questions — they're the easiest ones.
The blue ones are a bit harder, and the pink ones are the hardest.

1   Felipe wrote down how many blue, red and silver cars drove past his
    house at different times during one day. He put his results in a table.

	Red	Silver	Blue
Morning	23	36	12
Afternoon	15	23	18
Evening	15	13	12

a)   How many red, silver and blue cars drove past in the morning in total?

b)   How many more red cars did he see in the morning than in the afternoon?

c)   Which colour car did he see the most of during the whole day?

2   This table shows where pupils in a class would most like to go on holiday.

Country	Number of pupils
India	8
Spain	6
UK	4
Italy	3
USA	7

Draw a bar chart to show this data.

3   Gordon made some cakes on Sunday to sell in his shop.
    This bar graph shows how many cakes he sold each day for the next week.

a)   How many cakes were sold
     on Saturday?

b)   On which day did Gordon sell
     the lowest number of cakes?

c)   How many fewer cakes
     were sold on Tuesday than
     on Monday?

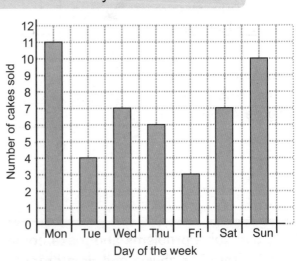

Practice Questions

4   Emma measured the temperature in her greenhouse at hourly intervals one afternoon. Her results are shown below.

Time	1 pm	2 pm	3 pm	4 pm	5 pm
Temperature (°C)	50	44	30	26	22

Draw a time graph showing this data.

5   Lori counted how many text messages she sent to her friends in a week and drew a pictogram with her results.

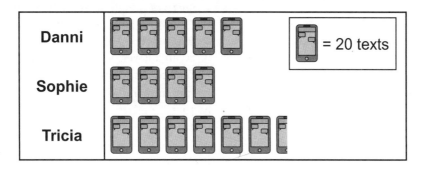

a)   How many text messages did Lori send to Tricia?

b)   How many more text messages did she send to Danni than to Sophie?

6   Ronan works at a harbour. He records the depth of the water over 12 hours and draws a time graph.

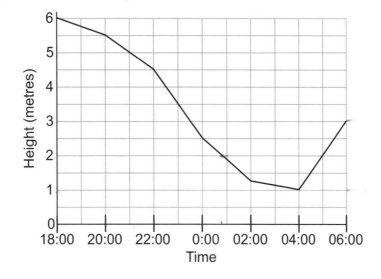

a)   At what time was the water at its shallowest?

b)   Estimate how long the water was less than 2 metres deep for.

c)   How much deeper did the water get between 04:00 and 06:00?

Answers

Pages 12-13 — Section One

1) 35, 42, 49
2) 2000, 3000, 4000, 5000, 6000
3) a) 1881
   b) 4465
   c) 9262
4) −7
5) a) 4
   b) 0
   c) 1
6) a) 3 thousands, 3 hundreds, 4 tens and 6 units
   b) 2 thousands, 5 hundreds, 8 tens and 7 units
   c) 4 thousands, 0 hundreds, 0 tens and 2 units
7) a) 8881
   b) 2259
   c) 589
8) a) 180
      176 is between 170 and 180.
      175 is halfway between 170 and 180.
      176 is more than halfway, so it's nearer to 180.
   b) 6000
      6359 is between 6000 and 7000.
      6500 is halfway between 6000 and 7000.
      6359 is less than halfway, so it's nearer to 6000.
9) 150, 175, 200, 225, 250
10) a) 55
    b) 9
    c) 24
11) −11, −8, −5
12) a) 500 > 459
    b) 619 < 691
    c) 1099 < 1100
    d) −5 > −8
       −8 is less than −5 because it's further to the left on the number line.
    e) −7 < 6
    f) 908 < 1160
13) a) 8000
    b) 7500
    c) 7550
    1000 less than 8549 is 7549.
14) a) 9.3 m
    b) Antony
       XI in Roman numerals is 11, and 11 > 9.3.
15) a) 5 °C
    b) 10 °C
       Remember to round up if the number is exactly halfway.
    c) −10 °C
       Because 15 is 3 × 5, you can count back from 5 °C in three lots of −5, so 0 °C, −5 °C, −10 °C.

Pages 22-23 — Section Two

1) a) $\begin{array}{r} 137 \\ +\ 22 \\ \hline 159 \end{array}$ b) $\begin{array}{r} 782 \\ +\ 441 \\ \hline 1223 \end{array}$ c) $\begin{array}{r} 2\overset{1}{0} \\ -\ 8 \\ \hline 12 \end{array}$

2) $\begin{array}{r} 56 \\ +22 \\ \hline 78 \end{array}$ So there are **78 vehicles** in front of Zoë.

3) $\begin{array}{r} 1\overset{0\ 14\ 1}{\cancel{5}\cancel{0}} \\ -\ 69 \\ \hline 81 \end{array}$ So **81** were girls.

4) a) $\begin{array}{r} 643 \\ +\ 391 \\ \hline 1034 \end{array}$

   So **1034** people went to the football matches.
   b) E.g. 643 is about 650, 391 is about 400
      650 + 400 = 1050
      So an answer of 1034 seems right.
      You could also use inverse operations to check your answer.
5) a) 12
   b) 48
   c) 7
   d) 9
   e) 3 × 4 = 12, 12 × 7 = **84**
   f) 8 × 2 = 16, 16 × 10 = **160**
6) $\begin{array}{r} 42 \\ \times\ \ 3 \\ \hline 126 \end{array}$ So the monkeys eat **126 bananas**.
7) a) 23
   b) 18
   c) 0
   A number won't change if it is multiplied or divided by 1. Any number multiplied by zero is zero.
8) 1 and 30, 2 and 15, 3 and 10, 5 and 6.
9) E.g. the opposite of addition is subtraction.
   So if Gideon is correct, taking 75 away from 267 should leave 182.

   $\begin{array}{r} \overset{1}{2}\overset{1}{6}7 \\ -\ 75 \\ \hline 192 \end{array}$ So Gideon is wrong.
10) a) Round 248 up to 250.
       Round 151 down to 150.
       250 − 150 = 100
       So **about 100** sweets are left.
    b) $\begin{array}{r} \overset{1}{2}\overset{1}{4}8 \\ -151 \\ \hline 97 \end{array}$ So **97 sweets** are left.
11) 1, 2, 3, 6, 9, 18
12) $\begin{array}{r} 9.79 \\ +\ 3.49 \\ \hline 13.28 \end{array}$ So Dave has spent **£13.28** in total.
13) $\begin{array}{r} 796 \\ \times\ \ \ 8 \\ \hline 6368 \end{array}$

Answers

14) $36 \div 4 = 9$.
So $360 \div 4 = $ **90 fish**.

15)
```
    2 7
  ×   4
  1 0 8
```
Nadia and her friends donate £108.
```
    ²⁷¹
  5 8 3
 −1 0 8
  4 7 5
```
So the charity still needs **£475**.

16) Number of jelly beans in each box:
```
    1 6
  ×   5
    8 0
    ₃
```
Number of jelly beans in total:
```
    8 0
  ×   3
  2 4 0
```
So James has bought **240 jelly beans** in total. It doesn't matter in what order you do the multiplication. If you did $16 × 3$ first you would get the same answer.

17) Large car parks:
```
    7 4 0
  ×     3
  2 2 2 0
      ₁
```
Small car parks:
```
    1 4 4
  ×     5
    7 2 0
    ₂ ₂
```
Total car parking spaces:
```
    2 2 2 0
  +   7 2 0
    2 9 4 0
```
A maximum of **2940 cars** can park in the town's car parks.

Pages 34-35 — Section Three

1) 3.4

2) a) $\frac{5}{11} + \frac{3}{11} = \frac{8}{11}$
b) $\frac{11}{16} + \frac{2}{16} = \frac{13}{16}$
c) $\frac{3}{25} + \frac{16}{25} = \frac{19}{25}$

You can just add the numerators together because the denominators are the same.

3) a) $\frac{9}{10} - \frac{3}{10} = \frac{6}{10}$
b) $\frac{8}{17} - \frac{5}{17} = \frac{3}{17}$
c) $\frac{19}{21} - \frac{11}{21} = \frac{8}{21}$

4) 11.2, 11.6, 11.8, 12.0, 12.1, 12.8

5) a) 10
b) 9
c) 17
d) 128

6) a) 0.8
b) 0.98
c) 0.75

7) $\frac{6}{18}$

8) $90 \div 10 = $ **9 people**
Jim divided his stickers into groups of 10, so to find out how many people he gave stickers to you need to divide by 10.

9) E.g.

$\frac{3}{8}$ of the circle are shaded in. The square is split into 16 parts. $16 = 8 × 2$, so you need to shade in $3 × 2 = 6$ squares. (Any 6 squares is correct.)

10) a) $\frac{5}{7} + \frac{4}{7} = \frac{9}{7} = \mathbf{1\frac{2}{7}}$
b) $\frac{11}{15} + \frac{9}{15} = \frac{20}{15} = \mathbf{1\frac{5}{15}}$
c) $\frac{6}{20} + \frac{19}{20} = \frac{25}{20} = \mathbf{1\frac{5}{20}}$

For these questions, you end up with the numerator being bigger than the denominator. You need to change the fraction to a mixed number by working out what fraction you're left with once you've taken a whole number away.

11) 11.1, 11.2, 11.3 or 11.4
All of these will round to 11.

12) a) $32 \div 4 = 8$
So $40 \div 8 = 5$
So $\frac{4}{5} = \frac{32}{40}$
b) $14 \div 2 = 7$
So $5 × 7 = 35$
So $\frac{2}{5} = \frac{14}{35}$

To find an equivalent fraction, the numerator and the denominator must both be multiplied or divided by the same number.

13) $122 \div 10 = 12.2$ cm. This rounds to **12 cm** to the nearest whole number.

14) E.g. Gerald ate: $72 \div 9 = 8$. $8 × 4 = 32$ tomatoes.
He gave his friend: $72 \div 9 = 8$.
$8 × 2 = 16$ tomatoes.
So Gerald has $72 - 32 - 16 = $ **24 tomatoes left**

15) $\frac{7}{7} - \frac{6}{7} = \frac{1}{7}$ So Abby has $\frac{1}{7}$ left.
$\frac{7}{7} - \frac{3}{7} = \frac{4}{7}$ So Rick has $\frac{4}{7}$ left.
$\frac{1}{7} + \frac{4}{7} = \frac{5}{7}$ So altogether they have $\frac{5}{7}$ left.

Pages 42-43 — Section Four

1) a) 1 km = 1000 m
So 3 km = $1000 × 3 = $ **3000 m**.
b) 1 hour = 60 minutes
So 4 hours = $60 × 4 = 240$ minutes
Add on 12 minutes: $240 + 12 = $ **252 minutes**.
c) 1 minute = 60 seconds
So 3 minutes = $60 × 3 = $ **180 seconds**.

Answers

2) a) 1 hour = 60 minutes
     So 2 hours = 60 × 2 = 120 minutes.
     Add on 10 minutes: 120 + 10 = 130 minutes.
     130 minutes is bigger than 120 minutes,
     so **2 hours and 10 minutes is bigger** than
     120 minutes.
   b) £3 = £3.00 = 300p
     300p is bigger than 260p, so **£3 is bigger**
     than 260p.
   c) 1 km = 1000 m
     So 1.8 km = 1000 × 1.8 = 1800 m.
     1800 m is bigger than 1500 m, so **1.8 km is
     bigger** than 1500 m.
3) Perimeter = 10 + 8 + 10 + 8 = **36 cm**.
4) Each square is 1 cm². The shape is made up of
   11 squares. So the area of the shape is **11 cm²**.
5) a) 299p
   b) 375p
   c) 25p
     This is the same as 025p, but you don't write
     the 0 in.
   d) 5p
     This is the same as 005p, but you don't write
     the 0s in.
6) a) 3 + 12 = 15, so the time is **15:45**.
     To change the time from the 12-hour clock to
     the 24-hour clock when it's afternoon, you need
     to add on 12 hours. You know it's afternoon
     because there's a 'pm'.
   b) 7:20 am
     Don't forget to add 'am' on to show that
     it's morning.
   c) 16 – 12 = 4, so the time is **4:30 pm**.
   d) 08:12
     It's morning, so you don't need to do much to
     change the time from the 12-hour clock to the
     24-hour clock — just add a 0 at the front and
     get rid of the 'am'.
7) Change the cost of the drinks into pounds:
   £1.25 = 125p.
   80 + 125 + 75 + 75 = 355p
   Change the answer back into pounds:
   355p = **£3.55**.
8) a) It's a square so all the sides are the same
       length (5 cm).
       Perimeter = 5 + 5 + 5 + 5 = **20 cm**
   b) It's a rectangle, so two of the sides are 9 cm
       and the other two are 4.5 cm.
       Perimeter = 9 + 4.5 + 9 + 4.5 = **27 cm**
9) a) It's 20 minutes past 2 in the morning, so the
       time is **2:20 am**.
   b) It's 5 minutes to 6 in the evening, so the time
       is **5:55 pm**.
   c) 22 – 12 = 10, so the time is **10:35 pm**.
   You've been asked to give your answers in the
   12-hour clock, so don't forget to add 'am' or 'pm'.

10) 1 year = 12 months
    0.5 year = ½ year
    ½ year in months = 12 ÷ 2 = 6 months.
    12 + 6 = **18 months**.
11) Break the time up into steps.
    E.g. 9 am → 12 pm = 3 hours.
    12 pm → 5 pm = 5 hours.
    5 pm → 5:30 pm = 30 minutes.
    Total time at work = 3 hours + 5 hours +
    30 minutes = 8 hours 30 minutes.
    Subtract the 1 hour he had for lunch:
    8 hours 30 mins – 1 hour = **7 hours 30 minutes**.
12) Change all the prices into pence:
    £2.25 = 225p
    £2.20 = 220p
    Add up how much Milly spent:
    225 + 65 + 220 = 510p
    Subtract this from £10:
    £10 = 1000p
    1000p – 510p = 490p
    Change this into pounds:
    490p = **£4.90**.
    You could also have worked this out by changing
    all the prices into pounds.
13) a) Each square is 1 cm long, so you can work
       out the length of each side.

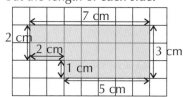

    Perimeter: 7 + 3 + 5 + 1 + 2 + 2 = **20 cm**
   b) Each square is 1 cm².

1	2	3	4	5	6	7
8	9	10	11	12	13	14
		15	16	17	18	19

    Area = **19 cm²**

Pages 52-53 — Section Five

1) kite
2) A and D — they are the only triangles with
   2 equal sides and 2 equal angles.
3) a) C, A, D, B
   b) B and D
4)

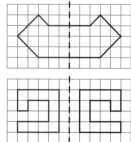

Answers

5)

6) Shapes B and C.

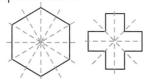

7) a) (7, 3)
   b) (6, 8)

8) This is a translation 2 squares right and 2 squares down.

9) (4, 2)

10) a)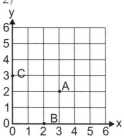

   b) (1, 5)

   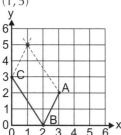

   Draw in the two sides of the parallelogram you're sure of. You know that parallelograms have two sets of parallel sides, so draw in lines parallel to the ones you've got, starting from points A and C. Read off the coordinates where these lines meet.

Page 58-59 — Section Six

1) a) Red cars = 23
      Silver cars = 36
      Blue cars = 12
      23 + 36 + 12 = 71 cars
      So **71 cars** drove past in the morning.
   b) Morning = 23 cars
      Afternoon = 15 cars
      23 − 15 = 8 cars
      So he saw **8 more red cars** in the morning.
   c) Red cars = 23 + 15 + 15 = 53
      Silver cars = 36 + 23 + 13 = 72
      Blue cars = 12 + 18 + 12 = 42
      So he saw the most **silver** cars.

2) E.g.

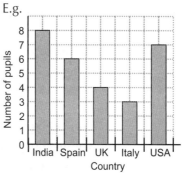

3) a) 7 cakes
   b) Friday
   c) Monday = 11 cakes
      Tuesday = 4 cakes
      11 − 4 = 7 cakes
      So he sold **7 fewer cakes** on Tuesday.

4) E.g

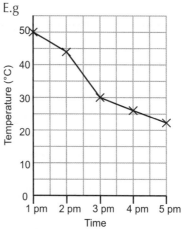

5) a) Tricia = 6 × 20 = 120
      120 + 10 = 130
      So Lori sent **130 texts** to Tricia.
   b) Danni = 5 × 20 = 100 texts
      Sophie = 4 × 20 = 80 texts
      100 − 80 = 20 texts
      So Lori sent **20 more texts** to Sophie than to Danni.
      Remember — each picture represents 20 texts.

6) a) 04:00
   b) It went below 2 m at around 01:00
      It went above 2 m at 05:00
      So the water was less than 2 metres deep for around 4 hours.
   c) At 04:00, the depth was 1 metre
      At 06:00, the depth was 3 metres
      3 − 1 = 2
      So the depth increased by **2 metres**.

Glossary

acute angles	Angles that measure <u>less than 90°</u>. They are <u>smaller</u> than <u>right angles</u>.
analogue	An analogue clock has <u>hands</u> to show the hours, minutes (and seconds).
area	The area of a shape is the amount of surface it covers.
axis/axes	The <u>horizontal axis</u> is the line along the bottom of a graph or chart. The <u>vertical axis</u> is the line up the left-hand side, running from top to bottom. <u>Axes</u> is the word for more than one axis.
calculate	This just means <u>work out</u>. It <u>doesn't</u> mean 'use a calculator'.
capacity	The amount of liquid something can hold when it's full. Capacity is measured in litres or millilitres.
centimetre, cm	A unit for measuring <u>distance</u>. There are 100 cm in a metre.
change (money)	The money left over when you buy something.
coordinates	Tell you the <u>position</u> of a point from the <u>origin</u>. They're always written in the <u>same way</u>, for example, (3, 4). The first number gives the position on the <u>x-axis</u> and the second number gives the position on the <u>y-axis</u>.
day	A unit of <u>time</u>. There are 24 hours in a day, and 7 days in a week.
decimal number	A number that's <u>between</u> whole numbers can be written as a decimal. For example, 1.7 is 1 plus 7 tenths.
decimal places	The places in a number to the right of the decimal point. For example, the number 4.56 has 2 decimal places.
decimal point	The dot you write in a decimal number. It comes between the units and the tenths.
degrees, °	The unit used to measure <u>angles</u>. For example, a right angle measures 90°.
degrees Celsius, °C	A unit for measuring <u>temperature</u>. The temperature inside a house is normally about 20 °C.
digit	A digit is one of these numbers: 0, 1, 2, 3, 4, 5, 6, 7, 8 or 9.
digital	A digital clock shows the time as numbers, for example, 08:30.
divide, ÷	<u>Share</u> equally or put into equal <u>groups</u>. For example, 6 ÷ 3 means 6 divided by 3, or 6 shared into 3 equal groups. (The answer is 2.)
equilateral triangle	A triangle with <u>all sides the same length</u> (and all angles 60°).

Glossary

estimate	An estimate is a <u>sensible guess</u> at the answer. You can use <u>rounding</u> to help you estimate answers.
factor	A whole number that divides exactly into another whole number. For example, the factors of 6 are 1, 2, 3 and 6.
fraction	Part of a whole number or shape.
frequency	How many times something happens.
heptagon	A flat shape with <u>seven straight sides</u>.
hexagon	A flat shape with <u>six straight sides</u>.
hour	A unit of <u>time</u>. An hour is 60 minutes. There are 24 hours in a day.
hundredths	The second digit after the decimal point. One hundredth is written 0.01 or $\frac{1}{100}$.
integer	Any whole number. It can be positive or negative. Zero is also an integer.
inverse	<u>Opposite</u>. For example, addition and subtraction are <u>inverse operations</u>.
irregular polygon	In an irregular polygon at least one side or angle is different.
isosceles triangle	A triangle with <u>two</u> equal sides and angles.
kilometre, km	A unit for measuring <u>distance</u>. 1 kilometre = 1000 metres. You can walk a kilometre in about 15 minutes.
kite	A <u>quadrilateral</u> with <u>two pairs of equal length sides.</u> It has <u>two equal angles</u>. None of its sides are parallel.
line of symmetry	If you <u>fold</u> a shape along a line of symmetry, the two halves <u>fit exactly</u> on top of each other. It's the same thing as a mirror line.
litre, l	A unit for measuring <u>volume</u> or <u>capacity</u>. Orange juice often comes in 1 litre cartons.
metre, m	A unit for measuring <u>distance</u>. 1 metre = 100 centimetres. A door is about 2 m high.
millilitre, ml	A unit for measuring <u>volume</u> or <u>capacity</u>. There are 1000 millilitres in a litre. A teaspoon has a capacity of about 5 ml.
minute	A unit of <u>time</u>. There are 60 minutes in an hour, and 60 seconds in a minute.
mirror line	The same as a line of symmetry.

Glossary

mixed number	A mixed number has a whole-number part and a fraction part, for example, 3½.
month	A unit of <u>time</u>. There are 12 months in a year (January to December).
multiple	Multiples are the numbers in a times table. For example, the multiples of 4 are 4, 8, 12, 16...
multiply, ×	The proper maths word for 'times'.
negative	Negative numbers are numbers <u>below 0</u>. For example, –1 or –10.
obtuse angles	Angles that measure <u>more than</u> 90° but less than 180°. They're <u>bigger</u> than a <u>right angle</u>.
octagon	A flat shape with <u>eight straight sides</u>.
ordering	Putting <u>in order</u>. For example, to order 3, 1 and 2 from smallest to largest, start with the smallest, then the next smallest: 1, 2, 3.
origin	Where the two <u>axes</u> of a graph <u>cross</u>. It has the coordinates (0, 0).
parallel	Parallel lines, faces and edges are always the <u>same distance apart</u>. They will <u>never meet</u> or <u>cross</u>.
parallelogram	A <u>quadrilateral</u> with <u>two pairs of parallel sides opposite</u> each other.
partition	<u>Split</u> a number up. You can partition numbers in many ways. For example, 173 = 100 + 70 + 3 or 173 = 150 + 20 + 3.
pentagon	A flat shape with <u>five straight sides</u>.
perimeter	The <u>distance</u> around the outside of a 2D shape.
perpendicular	Lines that meet each other at <u>right angles</u> (or would meet at right angles if you extended them) are perpendicular.
polygon	Any flat shape with <u>straight sides</u>.
quadrilateral	A flat shape with <u>four straight sides</u>.
rectangle	A <u>quadrilateral</u> with <u>two pairs of equal sides</u> and <u>four right angles</u>.
reflective symmetry	A shape has reflective symmetry if you can draw mirror lines on it.
regular polygon	In a regular polygon, <u>all</u> the sides are <u>equal lengths</u> and all the angles are the same.
represent	This just means <u>show</u>.

Glossary

rhombus	A <u>quadrilateral</u> with <u>four equal sides</u> and <u>two pairs of equal angles</u>.
right angle	A <u>quarter turn</u>, or 90°.
Roman numerals	<u>Letters</u> that the Romans used to <u>show numbers</u>. For example, V = 5 and X = 10.
rounding	Finding a nearby number that's <u>similar</u>, but easier to use in calculations. For example, to round 27 to the nearest 10, you have to find the number that's nearest to 27 <u>and</u> a multiple of 10. 27 is between 20 and 30 but <u>nearer to 30</u>.
scalene triangle	A triangle that has <u>no equal sides</u> or <u>angles</u>.
scale	The numbered marks on a line that help you measure things.
second	A unit of <u>time</u>. There are 60 seconds in a minute.
square	A <u>quadrilateral</u> with <u>four equal sides</u> and <u>four right angles</u>.
square centimetre (cm²)	A unit for measuring <u>area</u>. A square with sides of length 1 cm.
subtract, −	Take away one number from another. For example, '11 − 6 = 5' is '11 take away 6 = 5' or '11 subtract 6 = 5'.
tenths	The first digit after the decimal point. One tenth is written 0.1 or $\frac{1}{10}$.
translation	When a shape <u>moves</u> from one place to another <u>without rotating</u> or <u>flipping</u>.
trapezium	A <u>quadrilateral</u> with <u>one pair of parallel sides</u>.
triangle	A flat shape with <u>three straight sides</u>.
vertex/vertices	A <u>vertex</u> is a corner. <u>Vertices</u> is the word for corners.
week	A unit of <u>time</u>. There are 7 days in a week.
year	A unit of <u>time</u>. There are 12 months in a year, or 365 days.

Index